A Wreath of Golden Laurels

An Anthology of Poetry
by 100 Poets Laureate

Edited by
James P. Wagner (Ishwa)

A Wreath of Golden Laurels

Dedicated to the Poets Laureate of the past who have influenced the Poets Laureate of the present.
And to the Poets Laureate of the present who will inspire the Laureates of the future!

Foreword

What is a Poet Laureate? The two words certainly invoke something when heard. Perhaps it means something different to different people. But there is just something about that term, similar to the idea of Knighthood, that captures something in the imagination.

Like Knights, Poets Laureate come in all shapes and sizes, metaphorically of course. Some Laureates, have huge followings and can muster incredible crowds to their readings, others, people have only ever read on the page and never had a chance to hear live.

What exactly IS a Poet Laureate?

In the strictest of terms, a Poet Laureate is appointed by a governing body, or institution, usually for the purpose of composing poems for special occasions, celebrations, events, historic moments, etc. So, by this definition, is the Poet Laureate the supreme poet, that other poets as well as the public should look to for philosophical thoughts and poetic verse that capture the mind and the heart?

Of course, many Poets Laureate I have known have gone beyond the confines of simply writing verse themselves. Many have been college professors, teachers, workshop leaders, event organizers, publishers, editors, anthology compilers, and much more. Indeed, a large number of the Laureates I've seen have been builders of communities of poetry and beyond. Is that, then, the modern Poet Laureate's aim?

In ancient Greece, the Poets Laureate were crowned with a wreath made of laurels, in the same way they crowned those they considered champions. So, obviously, the title was held in great esteem to be put on the same pedestal as the likes of the heroes many poets were writing tales about!

We've come a long way from those days, or even the era where Petrarch was similarly crowned with a wreath many years later in the classical era in Italy. But many poets and literary fans have attended ceremonies, small and large, for the appointment of a Poet Laureate, and listened to the verse they had to offer.

This volume has poetry from over 100 Poets Laureate. We have Laureates appointed by towns, libraries, cities, counties, states, organizations, institutions, and more. The poets in this huge volume have different styles, different backgrounds, and come from different states and even different countries. But they are all Laureates. All of them have been appointed, by others, to share their work, their words, and their wisdom.

So we know the definition, but still, what exactly IS a Poet Laureate? The mystique of the title is something that has kept it relevant for thousands of years. Whatever magic the title brings, this volume is full to the brim with it. So turn the pages of this hefty volume, and step into a several thousand year tradition of poetic laurels.

~ James P. Wagner (Ishwa)

National Beat Poet Laureate of the United States 2020-2021
Long Island, New York Beat Poet Laureate 2017-2019

Table of Contents

Malaika King Albrecht

Heart of Pamlico, North Carolina Poet Laureate 2018-2021

The Way Desire Touches

Honeysuckle vines
slip blossoms
into the nests of herons.
We lose our shadows
in the widening dark,
and the sound of wings
is the wind shaking
radiance from the air.
Notice how vibration moves
through bodies like water,
how your fingertips
on my throat
make humming palpable.

Praise Song for What Is

Praise the frozen rain, the icicles daggering
the trees, the gray snow sludge. Praise
the shiver, the wet wind cutting through clothes,
the frozen water troughs. Blessed be
the hard frost, the frozen pond,
the apple sapling snapped in half.

Praise autumn and spring, the hot then cold
then hot again. Praise the corn mazes,
the haystacks, the reaping what we've sown.
Blessed be the fig tree, the honeycomb, the hive.
Praise the kudzu, the poison ivy,
the forsythia shouting yellow at a fence.

Praise the mosquito, the itch,
the scratch. Praise the heat waves,
the asphalt, the stopped
highway traffic. Blessed be
the dusty, the wilted, the dry
husks of corn in summer drought.

Praise the possum lumbering
into the chicken coop,
the fox slinking the wood's edge.
The owl, the hawk, blessed be
their swift descent to prey.
Praise the failures, the losses. Blessed be
the broken path that brought me here.

Malaika King Albrecht is serving as the inaugural Heart of Pamlico Poet Laureate. She's the author of four poetry books. Her most recent book is *The Stumble Fields* (Main Street Rag, 2020). She's the founding editor of *Redheaded Stepchild*, an online magazine that only accepts poems that have been rejected elsewhere.

J. Joy "Sistah Joy" Matthews Alford

Prince George's County, Maryland, Inaugural Poet Laureate

In Praise of Bridges

We honor bridges
And thank God for them
Created for such times as these
When firm footing is key
Allowing us to overcome obstacles
Avoid difficulties and disappointments

Each built and strengthened by ancestors
Elders, visionaries who predicted
And knew of our need

Together we build breath-taking
Awe-inspiring bridges
To carry our gifts
Even our burdens
As we lift more than our fists
To strengthen both builder and traveler

Short or long, fragile or strong
Bridges transport us
From that which has ended
To new plateaus and possibilities
That dwell, resonate and grow

Within our spirit, mind, and soul

Some will remain
Others will be
Carelessly or vengefully
Burned to the ground

So we build and cross bridges
That lift, guide, and empower us
Enabling both the anxious and the weary
To avoid stumbling block and valley
Offering safe passage
While deciphering signals
And warnings from yesterday's
Builders and travelers

So is our way directed
By these crossings cleared long ago
Showing us tried and tested ways
Toward our new and waiting tomorrow

J. Joy "Sistah Joy" Matthews Alford is the Inaugural Poet Laureate of Prince George's County, Maryland, and has authored three collections of poetry. She has hosted and produced the nationally recognized poetry cable television program, Sojourn with Words, since its inception in 2005. She has served as president of the Poetry Ministry of Ebenezer A.M.E. Church in Fort Washington, Maryland since 2003. She is the founder of Collective Voices, an ensemble of native Washington, DC poets known for their poems of social consciousness, empowerment, and spirituality. She lives in Maryland.

Donna Anne Allard

International Beat Poet Laureate for Canada

war musket grasses
(Bay of Fundy NB Canada)

i see no soldier's uniform
as i walk along these shores,
but fresh-blood cliffs, musket grasses,
& a labyrinth of our relics;
the unfolding of this puzzle,
to figure out a broader picture,
where rose clashed with fleur-de-lys
– an arcane coat-of-arms shared
by a friend. said to follow water-trails
like a pirate in search of a chest, as
magnet speaks closer to sand, he said
many have found treasures under the
sheet of their own graves. yet i favour
its peaceful clay to dyed denim & origin,
connecting with those who fell for their
flower, who sleep in this bay of mud. hooves
flirt in Fundy sun today, safe before my
watchful eyes, & I wonder if they passed
on the story to their offspring, when historic man
warred saddle to saddle. come walk with me,
sense the memories dancing in the tide like a

reverberating oratory along red cliffs & grassy
shores. then let us retreat from time & fog. i fear
ghosts & bell-walkers – they swear the land
still smells of powder.

go as a river

go as a river
be the keeper of the fallen limb
sea-dance, sun-worship
in O'Keeffe fluidity
dancing bones
loving bones
bones of love
root into short-lived tides
where even beach-faced inland spume
cannot break down a river's bones
as they resurface bygone lives
with unborn ones
rhythmic birth ripple...

go as a river

Donna Allard is a professional poet, member of the League of Canadian Poets, Writers Union of Canada, Canadian Authors Association, Ohio Poetry Association, and in 2019 she was awarded 'International Beat Poet Laureate for Canada' by the National Beat Poetry Foundation Inc. CT USA. She was a three term former President of The Canadian Poetry Association and is a former member of the Writer's Federation of NB. In 2014 Donna was given a position as Honorary Member in the CCLA (Canada Cuban Literary Alliance) by President Poet Laureate Richard Grove. After thirty years of being published across Canada and Internationally her writing has been translated into Greek, French, Shetlandic and Bengali. 'From Shore to Shoormal', Donna's first book by a trade publisher, co-authored with Shetland Island poet Natalie Hall (Brokenjaw Press, 2013), is in English, French and the nearly lost Old Scot/Shetland dialect. She resides down a long dirt road and lives in a 1909 homestead where muses fill her world with flowing visual poetry. Her official website is https://canadianbeatscene.wixsite.com/donnaallardpoet

Michael Amitin

International Beat Poet Laureate 2020-2021

Boatman's Elegy

Her hand cold with the death of romance
obligatory touch
we watched the chill settle like a mountain
chipped away by cheap time-square watch winds
irretrievably sad-

Still the flowers roll out, the cards keep turning
quick peck kisses, morning mist goodbyes
red heart valentine needle- shooting shared history
through warm nostalgic veins as
dark radio rains threw branches
against the Chopin windowpanes

Forever stuck in this merry, soul-mate long-play quick-riff affair
nightfall- sleep cascades.
Death Valley molten cliffs
Mr Fantasy stands stroking his quiff
barking carnival noise
into the oceans of space and joy that undulate between us
in our king size ruby-eyed forgotten sunken ship bed

So bake that candelight dinner
toss that last-ditch lingerie
we're old war buddies now
purple contented hearts

Poet and musician, Michael D. Amitin travelled the roads of the American West from California- east through the smoky burgs and train depot diners of Western Colorado, where he lived before moving to Paris, France. Recently named International Beat Poet Laureate 2020-2021, Amitin's poems have been published in California Quarterly, Poetry Pacific, North of Oxford, PoetryontheLake, Love Love Magazine and others. A current collaboration with Parisian photographer Julie Peiffer has given rise to the "Riverlights" project. and can be found at Riverlights.art

David B. Axelrod

__Suffolk County, NY Poet Laureate Emeritus__
__Volusia County, Florida's, Poet Laureate 2015-2023__

The Fabric

The fabric of the universe is
a silken cloth but it protects us.

Some wear it as sackcloth,
rend their shirt to mourn.

Others pull tight the hooded
string hiding their ethnicity.

Only, DNA differs so little
between us, we are universal.

The fabric is tightly woven
though tiny threads pull bare.

Our politics, religions are
hardly wrinkles in space-time.

As if skin color or the right church
makes us a better tailor.

From the fabric of the universe
    no flag need be woven.

Spring Chickens

On their 65th Anniversary.

1.
He hovers over her, a rooster
not afraid to be a mother hen.
At their age, you'd think
they'd be walking on egg shells,
but there's nothing chicken
about them, though they both
admit, "aging is not for the meek."

2.
After sixty-five years together
they still live free-range lives,
out on the town. See them walking
arm and arm, kissing publicly,
cracking jokes, tickling each
other's fancy. No egg on these
faces. No one can coop up this love.

Dr. David B. Axelrod, was Suffolk County Long Island's and is now Volusia County, Florida's, Poet Laureate appointed for 2015-2023. For his third Fulbright, he was the first Poet Laureate in the People's Republic of Chine. His twenty-third book of poetry—is *Mother Tongue*. Read more at his website: www.poetrydoctor.org.

JoAnn Balingit

Delaware's Poet Laureate 2008 to 2015

History Textbook, America

I'd search for Philippines in History class.
The index gave one page, moved on to Pierce.
The Making of America marched past
my enigmatic father's place of birth.
The week he died some man we didn't know
called up. *This is his brother,* one more shock,
phoning for him. "He died three days ago."
The leaden black receiver did not talk.
My uncle never gave his name or town,
we never heard from him. Was it a dream?
The earpiece roar dissolved to crackling sounds,
a dial tone erased the Philippines.
And yet my world grows huge with maps, crisscrossed,
my history alive with all I've lost.

from *Words for House Story* (WordTech Editions, 2013) by JoAnn Balingit

Words for House Story

after Li-Young Lee

So another word for mother is *narrate*.

Listen, thinks Narrate, as she sweeps
light into corners. She sees that
the windows are open. Narrate
likes to nest her hands
at the kitchen window for comfort.
She likes the bird that rings like a telephone.

Narrate needs the wind to feel at ease
again. She decides to leave the sand
on the floor. She looks high and low,
helps curtains relax, doors
to swing open. Lays hands on
their shoulders. Says, "Breathe."

Sashay is another word for child. Sashay
darts around a corner. Narrate holds
some underwear. Books are falling.
Sashay is tumbling head first
down stairs and yells, "It's fun!"

Narrate says, "Listen, this is driving me crazy!"
Another word for listen is *I-don't-have-time.*
Her secret word for husband is also *listen,*
yet again, *I-do-not-understand.*

15

Sashay persuades the neighbor dog to ride
the bucket of his mini-backhoe. Dares
the sweet turtle into sleeping on the roof!
Sashay does a slow, inscrutable dance
round the bare corners of *karate chop*

another way of saying *a-daughter's-empty-room.*
"What happened in karate chop?" Sashay wants to know.
Narrate leaves the vacuum in the middle
of karate chop, tapes a lavender story
of paint chips down the center of one wall.

But it's hard for her in karate chop. Depressions
left in the carpet hit like fists. Suddenly, Listen
is downstairs saying, "I should change my name
to *Emphasize.* Do you know every light
in this house is on? I just don't understand."

Oh, Narrate knows: Listen spells out *decoy*
when he means the words for *need-you.*
But she worries. Some days, she cries
"Decoy!" when she stumbles on his love.

from *Words for House Story* (WordTech Editions, 2013) by JoAnn Balingit

JoAnn Balingit grew up in Florida and lives in northern Delaware. She is the author of *Words for House Story* (2013) and two poetry chapbooks, as well as poems and essays at The Rumpus, The Academy of American Poets, McSweeney's Internet Tendency, About Place Journal, The Common, Asian American Literary Review and Poetry Magazine. A 2019 Hedgebrook alumna, she is at work on a memoir. Dr. Balingit served as Delaware's poet laureate from 2008 to 2015.

Randy Barnes

Lifetime Honored Historian Beat Poet Laureate

Who Do You Love

It was Charley Patton on the beltway
told of Robert J howling like an agitated wolf
among peanut shells and cheap liquor death
all the fine suits and battered guitars
Highway 61 lifeblood escape route
and the late Roosevelt Barnes in gold accouterment
his throaty epistle causing backflow along the Mississip
                                        like an 1811 dream
when the hills waved like sheets in a windstorm
and fields covered in snow shellac cotton in August
air so buggy birds topple in mid-flight
their bellies so full of protein they sink like stones
                                        in quicksand
this in the backyard of a southern showdown
where a hot-oven sun becomes one with limestone
and locals gather to turn up the heat
gods and goddesses of slide and shimmy
gut-bucket mambo in ankle-deep mud
whiskey-eyed moonrise over the flats.

Insomniac City

Evaporation syndrome in the brain-pan
a collective of sugar scarfers on wheels
room for the armaments close to the vest
corn liquor flatulence under the heat lamps
a troupe of fly smackers and toad stompers
all professionals right down to their plastic clogs
get a grip there's commies in the trees
run a tremble through the maze and see who fades
lapdogs and goobers for the meth score
newsboys banging their flatteries into hand-helds
a grand evening of vitriol on a global stage
O how the Americanos can dance the duck'n'run
it's hunting season in insomniac city no license
                                        required.

Randy Barnes is a poet who lives on an island in the Salish Sea. He is the Lifetime Honored Historian Beat Poet Laureate, Washington State.

Joseph Bathanti

Poet Laureate of North Carolina 2012 to 2014

Brooks Brothers Shirts

Ten hours a day,
my mother hunched downtown
in Brooks Brothers tailor shop – fretting
cuffs and belt loops, pleats, vents,

button-holes, lapels into ruthless
wool suits, unthinkably expensive,
for men who spent their days unsoiled,
whose soft hands never raised a callous.

After she punched out,
caught the streetcar, and high-heeled home
two icy downhill blocks
from the Callowhill stop,

she often breezed in with packages:
icy broadcloth shirts she'd monogrammed
with my initials,
swathed in smoky silvery tissue.

The deep navy boxes piped in gold,
the gold band that bound them,
and in their centers
the Brooks Brothers coat of arms:

a golden ewe lowered on a sling
into a sacrificial grail –
the *Agnus Dei.*
My mother dressed me like a prince.

"Apparel oft proclaims the man,"
I'd one day read in *Hamlet.*
Those luscious shirts:
the forbidden glory of plenty

(of too much, really).
Every day with neckties and blazers,
oxblood penny loafers, the Princeton
wave that swooped my yearning brow,

I wore them to school: yellow, blue,
pink, charcoal and burgundy pin-stripe,
tattersall, blinding
ecclesiastical white.

I wore them to church.
I adored those shirts,
my immaculate patrician destiny.
My mother washed them by hand,

hung to dry in the winter sun,
spritzed with water from an Iron City pony,
then shelved them in plastic bags
overnight in the freezer.

She loved them as much as I did.
My father, a steelworker, a crane-climber –
he loved them too.
He didn't want me to get my hands dirty.

He wanted me to work for myself.
My mother ironed in the cellar
where my father shaved
out of an enamel basin with hot water

from the washtub, a small mirror
on a nail pounded into the block wall
he whitewashed every year.
On his work bench she stationed

a sleeve board for the long tedium
of the crease, true as a plumb line,
dabs of starch at collar and cuff,
shots of steam from the iron's black button.

Mother's needle-hand steered
the hissing wedge just shy of scorching
the frozen fabric (which is the charm).
My shirts were sharp enough to bring blood.

Monday through Friday school,
then Sunday, High Mass,
the shirts awaited me, dangling on hangers
from the cellar's copper ceiling pipes,

the six of them in a skirmish,
nudging one another in the darkness,
complicit in my certain future,
swaying slightly,

like a slow dance,
in the heat vent's tepid whisper –
at their throats the oval writ:
Brooks Brothers Makers Est 1818.

Boar

He preys over the carcass of a doe,
left in the autumn windrows.
Once, climbing Agnes Ridge,
I'd come across him in the blackberry:
abiding, carnal –
matted, shaggy coat,
stupendous head.
He could have had me.
He let me know as much:
ancient face, haunted leer –
near smile.
There would be no mercy.
Today he see-saws on his haunches,
as he strips the doe:
his bestial gorge and groan,
tugging her up like taffy.
Finished, he rears and faces me –
safe, in mid-air, watching
from the balcony.
Cold columns of vapor writhe.
Solstice clouds,
from Johnson County, Tennessee,
storm Snake Den Mountain.
What's wrought in this valley's beyond our ken.
This creature – charged out of Shakespeare,
tusk-sharpened sneer,
gut-string pig-tail, on his chest
a white pentagonal smear –
kin to werewolves.

Joseph Bathanti is former Poet Laureate of North Carolina (2012-14) and recipient of the 2016 North Carolina Award for Literature. He is the author of ten books of poetry, including *This Metal*, nominated for the National Book Award, and winner of the Oscar Arnold Young Award; *Restoring Sacred Art*, winner of the 2010 Roanoke Chowan Prize, awarded annually by the North Carolina Literary and Historical Association for best book of poetry in a given year; *Concertina,* winner of the 2014 Roanoke Chowan Prize; and *The 13th Sunday after Pentecost*, released by Louisiana State University Press in 2016. His novel, *East Liberty*, won the 2001 Carolina Novel Award. His novel, *Coventry*, won the 2006 Novello Literary Award. His book of stories, *The High Heart*, won the 2006 Spokane Prize. His book of personal essays, *Half of What I Say Is Meaningless*, is the winner of the 2014 Will D. Campbell Award for Creative Nonfiction. His novel, *The Life of the World to Come*, was released from University of South Carolina Press in late 2014. Two new volumes of poems are forthcoming: *Rising Meadow*, in collaboration with photographer, Houck Medford, from Horse and Buggy Press (Durham, NC), in 2021; and *Light at the Seam*, from LSU Press, in 2022. Bathanti is Professor of English and McFarlane Family Distinguished Professor of Interdisciplinary Education & Writer-in-Residence of Appalachian State University's Watauga Residential College in Boone, NC. He served as the 2016 Charles George VA Medical Center Writer-in-Residence in Asheville, NC, and is the co-founder of the Medical Center's Creative Writing Program.

Alan Birkelbach

Texas Poet Laureate, 2005

The Former Poet Laureate Said

that he had finally just had enough
of admirers puttering their way down the sidewalk

onesey, twosy, like lost flagellants,
with copies of his books in their hands.

They were always mewling and whiney,
waiting for him to appear on his stoop

to "Bless You, Bless You All."
He admitted he was too accessible.

When he was younger inspiration
was as common as meatloaf.

He could pretty much rub two sticks together
and make a poem out of it.

But the reality was that one day his Muse
died inside him and he was left to try and hold

his reputation together on momentum alone.
It wasn't, he said so much a matter of losing control

as if control getting up and taking a flight
one-way to Bolivia or some other god-forsaken place

where it's probably struggling right now
inside some mustached coffee-picker

who owns one shirt and two goats
and whose entire vocabulary rhymes with sangria.

But I noticed that even as the laureate talked
he worked the chicken on his grill,

and between the turning of each breast
there was an unspoken counted pause,

and the lines were laid in regular rows
that he would constantly write and rewrite.

Alan Birkelbach, a Texas native, is the 2005 Texas State Poet Laureate. He is a member of the Texas Institute of Letters, Western Writers of America, National Park Foundation, and The Academy of American Poets. He is a Spur Award Winner, two-time international Indie Book Award Finalist, winner of North Texas Book Festival Award, Pushcart Prize Nominee, editor for several editions of the TCU Press Texas Poet Laureate Series, winner of the Pat Stodghill Book Publication Award and winner of the Edwin M. Eakin Memorial Book Publication Award. His twelfth book, "The National Parks: A Century of Grace", with fellow Texas Poet Laureate karla k. morton, was published by TCU Press in November of 2020. They visited all 62 National Parks, wrote poetry and took photos, with a percentage of the sales from the book going back to the Parks System. This is to help culturally preserve our greatest treasures – our National Parks-- for the next 100 years.

Bengt O Björklund

__Lifetime Sweden Beat Poet Laureate__

this very moment I fall
with my heavy breath ticking
in the old memory basket
is since long overdue

the sun is mere light
to the old man
moving his brittle bones
in the shadows

the sharp light
that meets his eye
squander
in old echoes

so many steps to contemplate
jigsaw puzzles
in need of more pieces
call for him to ponder

a certain ceremony
of greeting the wounded earth
finds him lost in a struggle
to count for more than one

solemnity is his hideout
behind the shed of all fear gone
listening to the gossip
of the rolling emptiness at sea

there are birds in the aftermath
stoic men attempting
what no man has achieved
lonely women singing in the surf

old man by the pint
downs severity with hot futility
rendering night a glow
that will be gone by morning

Bengt O Björklund wrote his first poem in a Turkish jail in 1970. He wrote it in English because no one spoke Swedish. Since then he has five published poetry collections written in English and five in his native language Swedish. Bengt is also an artist, a percussionist and a photographer. In 2018 he became Sweden Beat Poet Laureate - lifetime.

Joyce Brinkman

**Indiana Poet Laureate 2002-2008**

Apology from the Poetry Judge

Guilt churns my restless sleep.
I didn't pick your poem.
I should have known
it was yours. It began
with drinking beer.

You drink beer, lots of beer,
but me, the teetotaler, well
I don't like beer, and
I don't like poems that
talk about drinking beer,
about making beer, about
growing a certain kind of
hops, about dark amber color
or stout, beer venders, or green
bottles vs. silver cans.

But you like beer, and you
write poems about beer, and I
should have known
that the poem about beer
was yours.

But, in my defense,
at least half of the poems
in the contest were
about beer.

Poetry Bugs

I write poems in my head
as I sweep the kitchen floor
living the answer to that question
people always ask when
they find you are a poet.

Poetic ideas scurry through the mind
like the countless black ants bombarding
the calico cat's dried tilapia crumbs
scattered across the chestnut-colored floor.

For my German mother
sweeping the floor paired with
brushing your teeth:
       you eat,
       you sweep,
       you brush!

Never the housekeeper she was,
I often leave crumbs for ants
to feed on, until the cleaning girl
comes to end the banquet.

I dislike killing ants
even more than I detest
sweeping floors. It's
always easier to let
someone else do your killing.

If I were a Jain, I would

carefully sweep them from
my path. Instead I, unintentionally,
lure them to their deaths with
treats until she sucks them up
into the black hole of her vacuum.

I sweep on, ignoring the calls to pen poems
coming from the insects of ideas scratching
at the floor of my brain. They never stop
arriving, but giving them a plate.
would be less messy.

Joyce Brinkman, Indiana Poet Laureate 2002-2008, believes in poetry as public art. She creates public-poetry projects involving her poetry and the poetry of others. Her poetry is on permanent display in a twenty-five-foot stained-glass window in an airport, in lighted-glass artwork at a library, and on a wall in the town square of Quezaltepeque, El Salvador. Her printed works include two chapbooks, *Tiempo Español,* and *Nine Poems In Form Nine,* and two books with fellow "airpoets" Ruthelen Burns, Joe Heithaus, and Norbert Krapf, *Rivers, Rails and Runways*, and *Airmail from the Airpoets*. Her recent books include the multinational, multilingual book *Seasons of Sharing A Kasen Renku Collaboration*, from Leapfrog Press and *Urban Voices: 51 Poems from 51 American Poets* from San Francisco Bay Press, which she co-edited with Dr. Carolyn Kreiter-Foronda. Joyce has received fellowships from the Mary Anderson Center for the Arts, the Vermont Studio, and the Indianapolis Arts Council. She is a graduate of Hanover College and lives in Zionsville, Indiana, with her husband and a cantankerous cat. She is a founding board member of Brick Street Poetry Inc, the producer of the poetry podcast "Off the Bricks" which can be heard on Spotify, Apple Podcast, and other podcast platforms and found through the Bricks Street Poetry website http://www.brickstreetpoetry.org/.

Richard Bronson

Suffolk County, New York Poet Laureate 2021-2023

Threnody for Charles Weidman

I have been shown...that you are the mother of five sons
who have died gloriously on the field of battle.
~ Abraham Lincoln

A West Side loft,
Hardwood floor –
Your studio, divided
By a gray curtain
Hung loosely on a rod.

We sat in rows
Of metal folding chairs,
A small audience.

Your troupe had withered,
Your name familiar now
Only to aficionados
Of the dance.

In a white T-shirt, black tights,
A wiry body, steel gray hair,
You spoke softly of your art.

What god
Possessed you

At the moment
An old man stepped behind
The curtain, returned
Transformed?

And as your voice rang out
From a reel to reel recorder
Reading Mr. Lincoln's letter to Mrs. Bixby,
Your silent body told us
Of his grief—
The death of her sons,
Sacrifice of war,
Its need.

Richard Bronson is on the faculty in the Department of Obstetrics & Gynecology and the Center for Medical Humanities, Compassionate Care & Bioethics of the Renaissance School of Medicine at Stony Brook University and a member of the Board of the Walt Whitman Birthplace Association. He has won the Poem of the Year Award of the American College of Physicians and was recipient of the *Leonard Tow Humanism in Medicine Award*. Dr. Bronson is currently the Poet Laureate of Suffolk County for 2021-2023.

Douglas Powell / Roscoe Burnems

Richmond, Virginia, Inaugural Poet Laureate

My Son, The Monarch

my son flutters
floats through the kitchen
arms out and no direction
Like a butterfly playing tag with its own shadow

This halloween a butterfly is what he asked to be

unprompted

he knows nothing of what society associates
with fancy colors and flutter
he just loves butterflies

do you know how hard it is to find a "boy"
butterfly costume
there isn't one (they're all meant for girls)
they are all flowy dresses   monarch gowns
fairy's turned, multi-colored insect.
but we bought one
satin orange and black
frilly bottom and
wingspan bright as summer

my son is three

36

doesn't know what a dress is
doesn't think it's girlie
only daydreams himself under the sun
and free from his chrysalis

my childhood,
boys couldn't be butterflies
boys sting
boys are wasps
i learned to wound or to be wounded
but never chrysalis

chrysalis hardens but births a rainbow
a chrysalis allows what's inside to become new
I was taught boys don't rainbow they scab
scabs harden but birth a scar
like boys can look healed but are always scarred

He was so fascinated by butterflies
I learned things like some wings are poisonous
ain't that a metaphor for a boy born into toxic
carrying it on his body
on his back
dangerous   when he just wants to be beautiful
wants to stop and smell the roses
my son always stops mid stride
admiring a flower
or sky,
or the beauty in just being alive
He is a kaleidoscope of emotions and always breaking free
But butterflies are easy to break

That is what scares me most
That some person will rip his angelic innocence
I learned when a human touches a butterfly's wing
it damages a million tiny scales
but, if you stay perfectly still long enough
a butterfly will rest on you

i am trying to soften my primitive hands
so he lives like a butterfly and doesn't die like a man
i admire his dance in his butterfly costume
As he twirl and boast,
plays with trucks and trains and little boy things

sometimes he will rest his face on my palm
as is if to tell me " thank you for giving me wings"
and all this happens while I'm still in my own shell
learning from him   how to be free.

Richmond Virginia native, Douglas Powell/Roscoe Burnems is a poet, published author, spoken-word artist, comedian, educator, father, and Richmond, VA's inaugural poet laureate, who has dedicated his craft to entertaining and educating. Performance poetry has afforded him the opportunity to enlighten and entertain crowds across the country; he's been seen everywhere from coffee shops, schools and universities, theaters, and arenas. In 2019 he added a TEDx Talk to his list of accomplishments, speaking at a TEDxYouth event in November of 2019. He is no stranger to community and youth engagement. He has been a staple in the Arts Education scene for years and highlighted arts integration as a host for Emmy Nominated VPM's The Art Scene. As a "slam poet" he has been a three-time southern regional finalist (2009, 2014, 2022), National Poetry Slam Champion (2014), NPS Group Piece Finalist (2018), two-time consecutive NUPIC/Underground Slam Champion (2019, 2022), ScreenTime Poetry Slam Season 1 Champion (2020), and Lake Eden Arts Festival Slam Champion (2021). He is the founder and member of The Writer's Den Poetry Slam team and collective. With Roscoe as a coach The Writer's Den has been consistently ranked third in the country (2022). As a poetry slam coach he also took the VCU poetry slam team to be ranked 3rd in the world (2018). In addition to the putting on poetry-based events and poetry slams, the collective -consisting of mostly poets, but also songwriters, bloggers, and visual artists- conducts writing and performance workshops for youth and adults. Douglas hasn't limited his passion to competitions. He is the author of three published works: Fighting Demons, Chrysalis Under Fire, and God, Love, Death and Other Synonyms. He has also been published in many literary magazines and journals, including: Freeze Ray Magazine, Flypaper Magazine, Scene & Heard, Into Quarterly, Beltway Quarterly, Drunk in a Midnight Choir, and Rise Up Review.

John B. Burroughs

National Beat Poet Laureate 2022-2023
Ohio Beat Poet Laureate 2019-2021

I Am Not Ready to Die

yet.

I am not ready to go gently
into Dylan's "good" night
while wannabe Blackwater
thugs crush kinfolk for cash in Portland
and maybe soon Cleveland.

I am not ready to die
before there is justice
for Sandra Bland
and Breonna Taylor.

I am not ready to let go
while white would-be masters
and their whelps
so wary of wearing masks
seem rapt with delight
at the thought of regurgitating
yesterday's noose in their fight
against Black lives mattering.

Oh the splattering!

I am not ready to rest on my laurels
worthless as they may be
while there is work to do
and while not a word
the President says is true
is true.

Believe me.

I am not ready to watch
my loved ones be ground
down into the Cleveland blacktop
by blackguards and blackshirts
issued forth from Washington
by the liar, cheat and
black heart in chief
who believes the police force
that killed 12-year-old Tamir Rice
the same Cleveland police force
that shot 137 bullets into unarmed
Timothy Russell and Malissa Williams
might need a little extra firepower
to carry out their black work.

I am not ready to die, friends
unless it is by your side in the fight
for fairness, for right
and for equal justice.

Why Not

I've wanted
to write you
another poem, but
all that's come
out is a list
of things I should
tell you before
you decide whether
to love me back
as though love
is a decision,
as though I chose
to feel this way,
as though you'd
love me even
without my list
of reasons
why not

John B. Burroughs of Cleveland is the U.S. National Beat Poet Laureate for 2022-2023 and previously served for two years as the Ohio Beat Poet Laureate. He is the author more than a dozen books including *Rattle and Numb: Selected Poems, 1992-2019* (2019, Venetian Spider Press). A dynamic performer who has wowed audiences from Oakland to New York City and myriad points in between, John has hosted numerous poetry events in the Greater Cleveland area and maintains the Cleveland Poetics blog and Northeast Ohio literary calendar at www.clevelandpoetry.com. Since 2008, has served as the founding editor for Crisis Chronicles Press, publishing over one hundred books by esteemed writers from around the world. Find him on Facebook, Twitter (@jesuscrisis) and at www.crisischronicles.com.

Terry E. Carter

**Medford's (MA) Inaugural Poet Laureate 2021-2023**

Fireside Chat

Standing in the middle of misery street
mournfully regarding a pile of charred wood,
ash, and damp soot.
My home was here...
my memories and my things,
my comfort and my peace.
There is nothing to grab hold of.
The fire was all consuming.
The devastation was absolute.
The aftermath is yet unfolding.
My heart was here...
my letters and my books,
my compass and true north.

Standing in the middle of smoldering ruins...
blocks and blocks of scorched earth,
wreckage and ruins.
Five-hundred year old oak and elm trees,
reduced to blackened bits of charcoal.
There are no smiling faces to kiss.
no kittens to cuddle,
no babies to tickle,
no neighbors we know by name and need.
Not numbers, not statistics...

community.
I can't find a hug that feels right.
The story has no happy endings.
My heaven was here...
my lesser angels and my faith,
my roots and my piece of the sky.

Standing with my daughters and my dog,
in a high school gym three counties away.
We are the lucky ones.
We heard the reports and made haste...
choked down the smoke and made haste,
saw the blazing menace and made haste.
Couldn't gather much more
than the clothes on our backs,
some stuffies and a tablet.
Crazy that I just digitized all the pictures,
our lives on a thumb drive,
on a key chain
in my pocket.

Standing for the lost and the fallen.
There was no fighting this.
Containment simply meant, on to the next inferno.
Rescue has become recover and identify.
Hope has become compassion and sympathy.
Tears are the only water in abundant supply.
Our friends suffered too.
Good friends that won't ever come home...
even if there was a home to come to.
There was no escape.
only rebar, rope lines, and resistance.
Despite the heroic efforts of

gallant legions,
Hell came, saw, and conquered.
The rains came only to mock us.

Standing at the corner of burnt visions and broken dreams...
nothing that we built remains...
Not. One. Thing.
Million dollar mini-mansions and modest capes, incinerated.
The observers come to assess and plan,
then leave, shaking their heads,
and wringing their hands.
Only the true servants stay.
They pray with us.
They hold us tight.
They help us to grieve.
This was their place too.

Neighborhood is in the heart.
We are still standing.
We are still standing.

Grace Cavalieri

Maryland Poet Laureate Emeritus

Can I Count On You

If I were lying in a boat in a wedding gown would you see me floating by
If I named a star after you would you lie in the grass looking up
If I lived in a white house would you come sit on my front porch
If I were caught in a bad dream would you please wake me up
If I had a plaid blouse would you help me button it
If I could jitterbug would you do the double dip
If I were a red cardinal would you hold out a sunflower seed
If I caught all the fireflies in the world would you give me a big jar
If the night nurse forgets to come would you bring me a glass of water
If I have only minutes to look at the silky moon will you come get me

Athena Tells the Truth

Athena tells the Truth
She does not know any better
That's the good thing about being mythological
She does not encounter or counter
She is smart— says
No one ever solved a problem by being dumb

Everyone forgets her but B+ students

Athena was not what they expected
tilting away from the back story of Greece
But if parallels must be drawn
then lift her out of sleep

Bring her back in 4 inch heels
And purple fingernails
Put her in my body
I'm not afraid to be forgotten

She needed everyone who ever died
So give her new feelings to feel –
Do not attack because she wins at archery
And let us forgive her for still wanting romance—

Grace Cavalieri is Maryland's tenth Poet Laureate. She founded, and produces, "The Poet and The Poem" now from the Library of Congress, celebrating 45 years on-air.These podcasts are going to the moon in the "Lunar Codex" launch via NASA. Her 26th book, forthcoming 2023 (The Word Works) is "The Long Game: Poems Selected and New."

Kalamu Chaché

East Palo Alto Poet Laureate

Always Cherish The Moments

A loved one dies.
The heart cries.
Living in sorrow,
You can't think about tomorrow.
Life has come to a standstill.
Sadness is all that you can feel.
A life that once shined bright
Has faded into the darkness of the night.
You feel that it will be hard to live again.
But, live is what you will do again
Because we are all made of a Spirit
That must serve a purpose of a greater benefit.
The departure of a loved one helps us to know
That death is how life must go.
Death, in the truest sense of reality,
Is a way for the Soul to be free.
So, always cherish the moments you got to share
With your loved one who is no longer here.

Poetess Kalamu Chaché came to live in East Palo Alto with her family from Brooklyn, New York in the mid-1960s. After graduating from high school in East Palo Alto and pursing a college education in Forest Grove, Oregon, she returned to her community and earned an Associate of Arts degree in Liberal Arts from Nairobi College in East Palo Alto, California. Chaché has been serving the City of East Palo Alto, Belle Haven community of Menlo Park, the greater San Francisco Bay Area, and beyond in numerous professional, executive, administrative, advocacy, and artistic areas of employment and volunteer services. A strong advocate and practitioner of activism, advocacy, and volunteerism, specializing in the areas of youth development and the Literary/Music/Performing Arts, Chaché works tirelessly for many causes, events, and programs to help bring The Arts closer to people's hearts.

Chaché has been serving as the East Palo Alto Poet Laureate since her community became the twentieth incorporated city in San Mateo County. She is the Author of three volumes of poems: *Survival Tactics*; *A Change Of Interest*; and *Survival Interest: A Collection Of Poems Revisited*. Additionally, as a long-time and noted Cultural Arts Activist/Advocate, Educator, Event Organizer, Performing Artist, Producer, Promoter, Publisher, Songwriter, Vocalist, and Writer, Chaché is also a Vocal Recording Artist who appears on a total of six record projects with the Sons and Daughters of Lite and Daughters of Lite for Ubiquity Records and as a Solo Artist for Undercurrent Records and SONWA Records. Most recently, she founded and is offering an annual WordSlam Youth Poetry Contest in an effort to get more young Poets in her community seated at the Poetry table.

Liz Chang

Montgomery County. Pennsylvania Poet Laureate 2012

A Herd of Elephants is Sometimes Called a Memory
for A, who once alleged I remember too much of him

If our knowing of each other
were an earthly thing, it would be

dappled elephant hide,
ancient pachyderm's skin

stretched taut across
mud-cured foot pads

to receive tiny seismic
seizures like tender pen-taps—

calls to rejoin the herd
so low, they rumble

unheard past any human. I know
that your marriage is dying. I wish

to have language strong enough
to carve away the sorrow,

to mourn together and so low
that only we can hear it.

[previously published in Chang's chapbook *Animal Nocturne*, 2018]

Sighting the Rare Suburban Hyena

One afterlight car ride in my childhood,
we passed a roughened, mangy beast—
an apparition loosely draped in dog's clothing.

My mother, who was driving
and had a better view of the world,
declared our specimen "hyena."

I knew that wasn't right,
but she believed, hunted radio news
of cavorting zoo animals,

circus fugitives. The absence
of easy explanation cooked
a marrow-filled bone for storytelling.

If I brush that afternoon one way,
I see wildness stepping through
a clawed tear in our routine—

intentional, once she chose the path
that drove us there, recklessly
opposing her parents'

proffered name for me: "mongrel."
That wildness exposed
furtive ways of being in the world

a mother might not understand,
since the miracle of urban coyotes
is that they exist at all.

If I brush this scene back the other way,
the fine hairs of my hackles curl.
So much of my youth

wrongly christened,
and my mother, steering,
giving name to only her experience.

[previously published in Chang's chapbook *Animal Nocturne*, 2018]

Liz Chang was 2012 Montgomery County Poet Laureate in Pennsylvania. Her 2018 chapbook *Animal Nocturne* is available from Moonstone Press. Chang's poems have appeared in Verse Daily, Rock & Sling, Origins Journal, Breakwater Review and Stoneboat Literary Journal, among others. Her translations from French appeared in The Adirondack Review. She is the Visiting Professor of Creative Writing at Moravian University.

Teresa Mei Chuc

Poet Laureate Altadena, California 2018 to 2020

Names

I am tired of having five different names;
Having to change them when I enter

A new country or take on a new life. My
First name is my truest, I suppose, but I

Never use it and nobody calls me by this Vietnamese
Name though it is on my birth certificate –

Tue My Chuc. It makes the sound of a twang of a
String pulled. My parents tell me my name in Cantonese

is Chuc Mei Wai. Three soft bird chirps and they call
me Ah Wai. Shortly after I moved to the U.S., I became

Teresa My Chuc, then Teresa Mei Chuc. "Teresa" is the sound
Water makes when one is washing one's hands. After my first

Marriage, my name was Teresa Chuc Prokopiev.
After my second marriage, my name was Teresa Chuc Dowell.

Now I am back to Teresa Mei Chuc, but I want to go way back.
Reclaim that name once given and lost so quickly in its attempt

to become someone that would fit in. Who is Tue My Chuc?
I don't really know. I was never really her and her birthday

on March 16, I never celebrate because it's not my real birthday
though it is on my birth certificate. My birthday is on January 26,

really, but I have to pretend that it's on March 16
because my mother was late registering me after the war.

Or it's in December, the date changing every year according to
the lunar calendar – this is the one my parents celebrate

because it's my Chinese birthday. All these names
and birthdays make me dizzy. Sometimes I just don't feel like a

Teresa anymore; Tue (pronounced Twe) isn't so embarrassing.
A fruit learns to love its juice. Anyways, I'd like to be string…

resonating. Pulled back tensely like a bow

Then reverberate in the arrow's release straight for the heart.

"Names" appears in *Keeper of the Winds* (Foothills Publishing, 2014)

Former Poet Laureate Editor-in-Chief of Altadena, California (2018 to 2020), Teresa Mei Chuc is the author of three full-length collections of poetry, *Red Thread* (Fithian Press, 2012), *Keeper of the Winds* (FootHills Publishing, 2014) and *Invisible Light* (Many Voices Press, 2018). She was born in Saigon, Vietnam and immigrated to the U.S. under political asylum with her mother and brother shortly after the Vietnam War while her father remained in a Vietcong "reeducation" prison camp for nine years. Her poetry appears in journals such as *Consequence Magazine, EarthSpeak Magazine, Hawai'i Pacific Review, Kyoto Journal, Poet Lore, Rattle* and in anthologies such as *New Poets of the American West* (Many Voices Press, 2010), *With Our Eyes Wide Open: Poems of the New American Century* (West End Press, 2014), *Truth to Power* (Cutthroat, 2017), *Inheriting the War: Poetry and Prose by Descendants of Vietnam Veterans and Refugees* (W.W. Norton, 2017) and *California Fire & Water: A Climate Crisis Anthology* (Story Street Press, 2020). Teresa is a graduate of the Masters in Fine Arts in Creative Writing program (Poetry) at Goddard College in Plainfield, Vermont and teaches literature and writing at a public high school in Los Angeles.

Lorraine Conlin

Nassau County Poet Laureate Emeritus 2015-2017

First Stroking

How will you pose me
a warm intimate scene
evocative, demure,
silk robed or nude
lying on a bed of desire
between candlelight and dawn

Will you capture the
small curves of my back
nubile breasts,
my Rubenesque belly

Stroke me with charcoals
portray feelings of shape
a sculptural quality,
statuesque

Will you shade me with pastels
give me lean expressive lines
soft tones, solid shading
stroke shadows across my body
hatched reflections, rugged realism

or touch my form with sensuous lines
until I come to life

Will I be all you want me to be, *Mon Artiste*
Mon Amour

We Never Made It to Nova Scotia

Extreme weather cancelled the Blue Nose ferry,
washed out roads across the of Bay of Fundy
altering his well-planned journey,
the maiden voyage in our 1970 VW camper.

I mapped out a new destination
chose only blue roads,
those less-traveled back roads,
local highways and byways.

Storm warnings overnight at the wilderness campground,
arguing in the morning where to go for breakfast,
his choice a bakery nearby.
He went in to get coffee and sweet rolls
I fled across the rocky bluff
 to view the Bay from the smooth shore.

As I firmly planted my bare feet in the shifting sand
I was surrounded by remains of the outgoing tide,
tiny creatures and crustaceans stranded in crevices.

Now an incoming tide changing everything again
leaving no trace of what was
reached my knees swiftly and silently
in just minutes.

In the vastness of sea, sky and shrinking shore
I began to drown in tininess
wondering where I would go from here.

Lorraine Conlin is the Nassau County Poet Laureate Emeritus (2015-2017) Vice-president of the NCPLS and Events Coordinator for PPA. She hosts weekly Zoom poetry workshops poems have been published nationally and internationally in anthologies and literary reviews.

Paula Curci

**Nassau County, New York Poet Laureate 2022-2024**

I Choose NOW

I choose NOW!
Where my voice can speak without a fine.
Wherever, my body is still all mine.
Where I can travel in my own car.
Wherever, the Sentiments are.

I choose this moment!
Because yesterday we had no voice,
and woman starved to vote for choice,
and NOW our tomorrow can be taken from us.

I choose NOW!
Where I am not done yet.
Wherever, I can roam without a threat.
Where I can share equal space.
Wherever, I can plead our case.

I choose to be here,
but fear, that forevermore
the world before
will become now,
before our eyes, somehow.

When, is the end of NOW?
The minute we feel that feeling
thinking we've broken the glass ceiling
only to find - we've fallen through the floor
                    •   after the dance.

Paula Curci is the Nassau County Poet Laureate (2022-2024). She produces Calliope's Corner - The Place Where Poets and Songwriters Meet & What's the Buzz ® on WRHU.ORG. She co-founded The Acoustic Poets Network™ and is a retired counselor. Her Posics ™ style poetry is found on streaming services.

Lori Desrosiers

<u>National Beat Poet Laureate, United States, 2016-2017</u>

All we need is music

I try to be still
but my body won't let me.
First my shoulders
shimmy to the beat
then my arms let go
the chair and my hips
propel me to movement
on a rug, a supermarket aisle
or a dance floor.

Doesn't matter
what kind of music,
Latin, Zydeco, R & B,
all of us move together
every race, religion,
political affiliation
You can't tell
what's on our minds
when bodies are in motion,
when the drums
carry us away.

The beat
is our deepest instinct.
To change the world,
all we need is music, really.

City People

We used to walk the streets of love, find bodies couched in sunless base-
ments and ratty lofts, there in the city of the 1950's when I was a small child
and the incinerators burned day and night, blackening socks and starched
white shirts of men with families on their way to work. Downtown the bums
on the bowery pissed in the same cobblestoned streets where Whitman used
to walk, and the warehouses still spewed smoke, the workers on Wall Street
smoked all day and the buildings seethed with cigarette ash and sweat. In al-
leyways sex workers and lovers snuck a kiss or a fuck, vendors laid out
blankets along the dirty sidewalks, hawking hats, bangles and worthless
watches to tourists who would spend the day looking up at the skyscrapers.
One day around 1968 I went to Chelsea and stood looking up on purpose,
watched while first one at a time, then In small groups, people looked up. I
left them there, heads craning to see nothing of significance, just the Octo-
ber sky and overhangs of ornate stone, the wrought iron balconies of down-
town brownstones.

Lori Desrosiers' books are The Philosopher's Daughter, Salmon Poetry,
2013, Sometimes I Hear the Clock Speak, Salmon Poetry, 2016 and Keeping
Planes in the Air, Salmon 2020. Two chapbooks, Inner Sky and typing with
e.e. cummings, are from Glass Lyre Press. Poems have appeared in numerous
journals and anthologies. Publisher of Naugatuck River Review, a journal of
narrative poetry and Wordpeace.co, an online literary journal of poetry, fic-
tion, non-fiction and art in response to world events. United States Beat Poet
Laureate 2016-2017.

William F. DeVault

National Beat Poet Laureate, United States 2017

Xochiquetzal

your breath is intoxicating evidence that you are alive
and as it quickens it amplifies life to a sacred mystery
to be untangled as we tangle like writhing lithe liars
speaking the truth only with flesh and inner spirits
released in the task caskets of our transfigurations.
veils sail away in a shower of flowers, butterflies
and the manifold marigolds strewn in your path.

ruby blue and true, blood floods and courses,
forces we cannot deny try as we might to fight the surrender,
pretender to a false immodesty. transcendent precedents
swept from the table as soon as we are able
to catch our breaths and affirm our deaths
in a celebration of a thickening taste we placed
like communion wafers of an intimate religion.

leave no stone unturned, our band and brand is burned
into the cracked and sacked altars stacked high in our inquiry,
our diet of wyrms wherein we throw down our theocricide
ride our preferred angels into the heavens
on until morning becomes another charade parade
of the pretense of civilization we shed last night.

William F. DeVault is the author of over 32,000 poems extant (he throws away the ones he does not like) and was called "the Romantic Poet of the Internet" by Yahoo! in 1996 as well as being the US National Beat Poet Laureate for 2017-2018. He has currently 28 books to his credit, including his massive *The Compleat Panther Cycles* (643 poems), numerous anthologies, and 5 CDs of his performances, as well as being occasional lyricist for European industrial artist Ophidian. He tours the United States from Boston to Los Angeles, from New Orleans to Detroit. In 2015 he was authorized to record Allen Ginsberg's legendary "Howl" by Ginsberg's estate, which can be found in his podcast for August 16, 2015. He has 2 ex-wives and three magnificent children.

Rosemarie Dombrowski

Phoenix, Arizona, Inaugural Poet Laureate

Prison Blues

Twenty weeks later
and I've lost another man.

The train cars are poems
moving across the delta.

I can't stop thinking
about the fact that
7 out of 1000 people
are incarcerated.

I can't stop loving them
despite the risk.

Breast Cancer Blues

What physical bodies
have we ever really owned,
land or otherwise?

My friend's sister is dead.
My friend's breasts have been
sliced from her body.
The poets write poems
on the eve of lumpectomies,
in the hours following surgery,
in the days after returning to work.

I skip my mammogram
for the twelfth time
because radiation is a plague
and I'd rather meditate.

Rosemarie Dombrowski (RD) is the inaugural Poet Laureate of Phoenix, AZ, the founding editor of rinky dink press (a publisher of micro-poetry collections), and the founding director of Revisionary Arts, a nonprofit that facilitates therapeutic poetry workshops for vulnerable populations and the community at large. RD has published three collections of poetry to date and was the winner of the 2017 Split Rock Review chapbook competition. She's the recipient of an Arts Hero award (2017), a Fellowship from the Academy of American Poets (2020), a Great 48 award (*Phoenix Magazine,* 2020), and the Arizona Humanities Outstanding Speaker Award (2022). In April 2022, she gave a TEDx talk entitled "The Medicinal Power of Poetry." Currently, she's an Assistant Professor of Practice at U of A Biomedical (Phoenix) and a Principal Lecturer at Arizona State University, where she specializes in medical humanism/medical poetry, literature of the marginalized, and journal editing/production.

Carlos Raúl Dufflar

New York City, Beat Poet Laureate, 2020-2022

Sitting Besides the Summit

The footpath into the woods
The trees were tall as I pass
besides tree trunks that have fallen
when the wind was speaking
The air is sweet and not far but near
The grass is green
And embracing Pachamama
The sounds of life of sunshine beams
While the lake lays still
Far below the chipmunks
run wild over the rocks
and the squirrels are not far behind
With laughter and a smile
A space which is a hidden beauty
Sunflowers are growing wild
so close to you
while the water drops and flows
from the waterfall
And today on this hour
We must remember Jimi Hendrix
and that funky guitar
Stone Free 52 years ago
from the Puget Sound
from a Band of Gypsys

The Beat Poet waits for the sunlight
To shine at every corner
Laying beneath Inti is a native sun

Carlos Raúl Dufflar is the New York City Beat Poet Laureate 2020-2022. He is a member of the Academy of American Poets and the Edgar Allan Poe Society of Baltimore.

Peter V. Dugan

**Nassau County, New York, Poet Laureate 2017-2019**

Beatification

I am one of those lost souls, the last generation destroyed by
madness, pent-up frustration and teenage angst. I sauntered
down sleepy suburban streets to hang out at strip-malls,
shopping centers, burger joints, and pizza parlors. Bar
hopping, bike riding and park jumping from Ally Pond to
Forest Park just looking for a buzz or something better to do.
I made a great escape into the city. Shuffled down to Union
Square got high, caught rock & roll shows at the Palladium,
and drank at Max's Kansas City. I became a barbarian on
barbiturates, drowning in shots of bourbon and bottles of beer,
stumbling down the road to Washington Square. Dealing with
the cock-slingers, cocksuckers, and mother-fuckers who sell
snow to Eskimos. Popping pills for thrills, coke, crack, smoke
and smack, mounted the great white horse a black knight
chasing the dragon for nights on end. With an unconditional
surrender, I gave up the quest to nowhere and found serenity
on St Marks Place. A sense of spirituality tempered by reality,
science and psychology, shunned organized religion, a mixture
of fact, fiction and fantasy, pseudo-intellectual mythology that
passes as absolute truth. I trucked on down to W 12th Street,
spent a couple of years at my old school learning something
new. Reading, writing and listening evoked my words to flow
on to paper, stories and tales, views and vistas, prose and
poetry. Words became my salvation, a metamorphosis of

being. Now I stand on the corner of Joey Ramone Place down the block and across from the Bowery Poetry Club. CBGBs is gone, replaced by a clothing store. Joey is rolling over in his grave or is he laughing on how things have changed, but remain the same. I cross the street, notice my name scrawled on the chalkboard outside the Poetry Club, a feature for the Beat Hour. Inside the picture of Allen Ginsberg with bushy black hair, beard, glasses and Uncle Sam top hat looks down smiling. It's all cool and I'm finally here.

Modern Americana

This is the land of freedom of choice:
Coke or Pepsi,
light beer or dark,
less filling, tastes great,
Republican or Democrat,
horse manure, cow manure,
different crap,
same smell.

America is now a pie
divided into eight slices,
but, there are twelve at the table,
and three of them want seconds.

It's all a game.
George and Martha never had a son.
Truth and illusion;
it doesn't make a difference,
we still sit in the waiting room
expecting delivery.

Money is the new Messiah,
greed is the national creed,
"In G-O-D (gold, oil &dollars) we trust,"
but, credit cards are accepted.
The government of the people
has been bought and sold.
It's strictly business,
nothing personal.

The heart of America
stopped beating,
the blood clotted,
no longer red,
now medi-ochre,
and pumped
by the pacemaker
of public opinion.

And still there are those that believe
that the only real American patriots
are true blue and white
or least act white,
and all the stars
are in Hollywood.

Peter V. Dugan is former Nassau County Poet Laureate, NY (2017-19). He has published seven collections of poetry and co-edited four poetry anthologies. He has many awards most notably, being twice nominated for Pushcart Prizes 2016 for his poems: *Jesus Never Rode a Harley* & *Mile 0*, an Honorable Mention by The American Academy of Poets, for *Hey Bobby* (1994), The North Sea Poetry Scene Service Award (2008), and The Long Island Bards Mentor Award (2014). He has been a poetry judge for Long Island Fair 2019 and a regional judge for Poets Out Loud 2018-19-20. Mr. Dugan hosts the Celebrate Poetry reading series at Oceanside Library, Oceanside NY and is the co-founder of Words With Wings Press a non-profit poetry publishing company.

Joe Engel

__Kenosha, Wisconsin, Poet Laureate__

Your Turn

Light catches the coins on the floor
by the vending machines
in the corridor, don't look around
before you take them, before you slide them
down the dark throat of your pocket.

Remember, when the slot machine
swallows them, they were not yours.
If you win, it's not money earned.
It's just gold dust, deserved.
Call your wallet pollinated.

This might be your day.
Rewarded now for how you don't
betray peoples secrets,
or ever call in sick. Trust me,
we see your smile

as the man at the dice table
wearing the Yankees hat loses a grand.
That's okay. And listen, on your lazy
ride home, do not gape at the sight
of someone's car burning.

Pass the smoke pluming from rubber
hoses without looking; those flames
want more than air and night. Do not
slow to watch like everyone else.
Who knows what luck is.

When you arrive at your flat
by the harbor and see
your land lord's half sunk dinghy,
remember the ten dollar bill
you almost chased into January waves;

how you could see it, twenty yards out
riding a slab of ice, rising and falling,
up and down in the water, and think,
before you call about the boat,
how you had to let it go.

Joe Engel is currently the Kenosha, WI poet laureate. He graduated from the
University of Wisconsin La Crosse with a bachelors degree in English. He
works as a custodian at Gateway Technical College so he can pay his student
loans among other things. He has been writing most of his life and has learned
to leap back and forth between fiction and verse. He is extremely honored to
represent his city and county as poet laureate. Kenosha has seen recent strife
and adversity, like much of the U.S. in 2020. He believes that anything can
be turned into poetry. And believes that is necessary.

Katherine Hahn Falk

Bucks County, Pennsylvania, Poet Laureate 2017

Hungry Ghosts

Ghosts may not be mentioned around Lily.
She is emphatic about that. She does not want to know
about anything she can't see.

After my friend Laurie's mother died,
her Tibetan Buddhist brother-in-law, Kunga,
said he was cooking for her mother so Laurie asked

"why? She's dead." "Ghosts get hungry too", he said.
Thankfully, every Buddhist Temple sets a place at the table
for the Hungry Ghost. Are there enough places

set for the number of ghosts? Do they share the offerings?
How much food and drink do ghosts want or need?
How do they use it? Where does it go? Do they drink tea?

I will cook for you if you go first. Day and night.
I will say the mantra three times, sit at the table with you
in case you're there during that bardo stage,

in between the day you leave your body
and when you go to begin your next life 49 days later.
Buddhist monks know where a person's next life will be.

They told Laurie that her mother would be the middle boy
in a family of three sons. It's said people choose parents
by the lessons they each need to learn.

Once only, in a big silent voice, I issued an invitation,
"Calling all souls. If there is a soul out there
that needs a body, come on in" . . . and Lily did.

For You

I cover my eyes with my right arm, a log
across water, a path to look for you,

in clear darkness that calms my breath,
that in its evenness shimmers.

Almost instantaneously, you appear
with an impish smile and classic white garb.

You're in a horizontal posture
not dissimilar to your position in the body bag

I asked be opened beyond the fraction of your face
they thought would do, your handsome face,

your beautiful hair, but your whole self,
lying there beyond sleep.

With my arm removed from its stance across
my eyes and us together back in the morgue, I cannot

help but wail in our bed, wail after you in the abyss
till I retreat back to your angel self, your wink,

the pucker of your lips as if for a camera
to say, "Come ahead, remember this."

Darkness overlaid with mottled threads of white film:
Your image no longer there. Your healthy hands

the way they looked in life now only in my mind (as I stress
and fight the image of your right hand after death),

your hands that could do almost anything
measure, construct, repair, doggedly, determinedly,

lovingly play guitar, knowingly lovingly play me.
I stand on a speck of space dust and look out on the vastness,

moments, seeming caverns, space refuge for you,
for you to suddenly re-appear.

Katherine Hahn Falk's poems have been recognized through publications and awards including an upcoming book, (Moonstone Press, 2021) and event commissions. She was Pennsylvania Poet Laureate for Bucks County in 2017. Recently, Katherine was one of four poets for *Radical Freedom: Poets on the Life and Work of H.D.* and she was an editor for *Fire Up The Poems*, an anthology of poetry prompts for HS teachers. Her work is also featured in the just published anthology, *Carry Us To The Next Well.* She loves working with students on their poetry.

Sandra Feen

Ohio Beat Poet Laureate 2022-2024

Not Buried

A tree thrives despite its narrow space
between the gray wooden fence, ending
the square purse of a backyard
on Woodette Road, and the still
bright-ugly chain link manacle
pocketing Columbus's new I-270.
A girl crouches under the tree in a spot
just large enough for ten-year old legs to fold,
knees propping a deep rust diary,
back pressed against metalwork.

She writes, brushes long braids that interrupt her
blue-lined small page, loves the outdoor secrecy
of a passion already unyielding, in this
her fourth-grade year.
Every sense of her lives, breathes scrupulous:
she is aware and not bothered by sticky skin,
a lady bug on forefinger, bees prompting.

She thinks she hears the sudden creak
of the back-screen door,
peers through her pretend barricade; a mother's
auburn head strains to see hers.
The mother calls for her. She must drop

this narrow-expansive corner of day
and unravel braids, make tight pin curls
wear purple gingham to sister's play.
She buries diary in a shallow grave
eager to retrieve it the next morning, drink
now quick momentum of family.

She knows she is different, so young
to relish writing as gift and enjoy
a sister's evening art.
This canvas paints contentment, but a flash
of dismal sky foreshadows.
She looks back at treasure's ghost under maple,
wistfully knows soul already too well,
wonders about decades of disruptions ahead--
ones that will not foster.
She reruns her course, climbs quick
over the intractable fence,
squeezes back to spot still word-warm,
erases leaves, clumps of dirt from
a vinyl cover marked with a red "top secret" sticker
and burgundy peace signs.
It could rain overnight.

Retired teacher Sandra Feen is a photographer and the 2022-2024 Ohio Beat Poet Laureate. She won *Heavy Feather Review's* 2021 Zachary Doss Friends in Letters Fellowship for her collaborative work with Rikki Santer, titled *Emotion Bus*. She has published three books: *Evidence of Starving*, *Meat and Bone*, and *Fragile Capacities: School Poems*. *Fragile Capacities: School Poems* was nominated for an Ohioana Book Award, and the poem "Palms Monday," a Pushcart Prize.

Doris Ferleger

**Montgomery County, Pennsylvania, Poet Laureate**

Love Letter from Time

I love the word *emergency*.
       Its redness, its lack of eventuality, its flash
            and crime. Its brothers—burn and rope.

I love the way humans startle,
       the jerk back of the body, the lunge forward.
          No sideways movements

come with emergency. No rhythmic beat or brush
       of drum begins it.
          Always the rigid riot.

Sometimes a pall of silence
       covers the body
          so it looks like the silvery sheet,

tissue light, tissue thin, is far less
       than volcanic.
          Emergency—

I like the evenness of its four syllables,
       how it takes too long
          to say it. By the time you say fire,

the house is rubble.
      By the time you say smoke,
            the sparrow, the tit-willow—

are hollowed out, featherless.

Crusts of Our Afflictions

We agree to meet on the footbridge
      after you've run and sweated for miles.

You place on your head
      the sky-blue *kipa* I've stolen

from synagogue this morning
      and the two of us tear,

into uneven bits,
      the ritual bread I've brought,

toss into the creek the crusts
      of our afflictions,

a year's worth
      of what some call sins.

Creek waters course, carry
      our regrets downstream

over sticks and stones.
      (I used to worry as a child

the fish might eat my sins
      and die.)

We recite the prayer of penance
      we each know, heart by heart,

year by year. This year you close

your amber eyes for a long time,

then look intently into mine—your deepest way
    of speaking

sorrow for the slight
    dent in the hood

over the stove that doesn't look like much—
    doesn't resemble a history—

except sometimes
    when the night winds blow terribly,

and moonlight leaks between roof planks,
    and a thousand crickets call—

I imagine we live in a ruined house.
    Afraid I have said or done one too many

mother things
    that have dented your heart.

As a child you used to sing:
    Sticks and stones

may break my bones, but words
    will always hurt me.

Today, on the footbridge
    on the first day of the Jewish New Year,

you say *September*

is a grieving month,

and I say perhaps it is
      grief that causes all discord—

grief left ungrieved—
      or is it a fear

of weeping—
      or a shame

of needing
      to know we are loved?

Doris Ferleger, former poet laureate of Montgomery County, and winner of the *New Letters Poetry Prize, Songs of Eretz Poetry Prize, New Millennium Poetry Prize,* and the *AROHO Creative Non-Fiction Prize,* among others, is the author of three full volumes of poetry, *Big Silences in a Year of Rain,* (finalist for the *Alice James Books Beatrice Hawley Award),* *As the Moon Has Breath,* and *Leavened,* and a chapbook entitled *When You Become Snow.* Her work has been published in numerous journals including *Cimarron Review, L.A. Review,* and *Poet Lore.* Aliki Barnestone writes of her work: *Ferleger's memorable poems keep singing with their insistent beauty.*

Alice B Fogel

New Hampshire Poet Laureate 2014-2019

The flowering

begins with fern and fungi   slow-growing palms
with gymnosperms spread

flowerless over the earth   begins
with the needle   fir spike   gingko   a seed

borne naked on cone scales and hatched
like the eggs of a lizard or bird   ·   the flowering begins

long after the exoskeletons of conifers
the armor of spruce and yew

cedar and juniper   begins
beyond eons of bristlecone pine present

before Siddhartha   tall before Jesus or Muhammed
through millennia   evergreen   wombless

grew nearly eternal without flowers   for still none
scented or surprised shadows under redwood   liana

or ephedra   yet somehow the flower
by chance or by design did arrive and then the holy ones

said *this is beauty for beholding*   *a practice*
a better self to contemplate like a navel   said

we must be like this lily   neither toil nor spin   we must be
a like becoming from within

and so they beheld and became and saw in the flower pure
being without purpose

even young Buddha in wonder misunderstood
the flower   cupped with his small fingers like stems

magnolia petals in his palm and said *peace*   and *love*
and in the sun the flower suffered

fools and went on opening   saying nothing
men could hear   but the whole world

after the flowering began
shifted

while pollen sifted over oceans to land
and xylem and phloem

fluted their solar and soiled blood   and sporophytes
from new ovaries of apple   hibiscus   and papaya

in their amniotic fluid like the embryos of mothered
mammals who now finally would flourish from this food

blew across distances on birdwing
and water and wind   pivotal   calamitous

blossoming fomented its revolution of fruit
tea and spices and opium and from these the crucial root

of desire began to grow like a rose
that is how it begins

the true bloom of human endeavor   wistfulness   war
trade and invasion   all civilization   and because

what flowers dies   the flowering
is how we began   to end

[previously appeared in Green Mountains Review and in Archaeopteryx]

Georgic

"This is what the soil teaches: If you want to be remembered, give yourself
away."
    —William Bryant Logan, *Dirt*

Soil is—romantically or not, as you wish—stardust. Everything
on earth is stardust. Earth itself is spun stardust, and all dirt
is an immigrant. Its flotation through the universe
traces the shapes of the forcefields—gravitational, magnetic,
kinetic—sphere, spiral, web—dust is taken by.
First—the rains, the sea, salt, minerals. Then bacteria, color—
then fungi and molds crusting into a skin—
envelopes of land and life containing sea, setting creatures free.
Dirt performs its own forces too: in the delta,
the flocculated benthic soils seethe in a teaspoon
with a greater diversity of organisms—more than 7 billion—
than people number here on earth. These and the land
growing food for the masses store 3 times the carbon dioxide
than the atmosphere can. Dirt is communal. Dirt is the soul
and the body of the earth. Soil is global: winds
carry loess upward and drop it 1000 miles away. Africa moves
to South America, Israel to Iran. Soil turns prairie
into forest, writing its name in the four elements
on its profile and in its substrates and transforms
material into organic life and death. Nowhere
is there not the teeming, industrious, symbiotic machinations
of the living—or the finished dead, the buried bodies—
collaged from decay and the stillness that descends to dirt.
Made of maple leaves, of antelope bones, of your house one day,
of you—dirt will organize itself into a memorial, a source,
alluvium, strata. Volcanoes spewed minerals in lava and ash

to the surface—and that was more dust. Glaciers
migrating and melting powdered mountainsides—more dust.
And now after this dust of so much has decomposed for millenia,
we step over its buried treasure, breathing in
the timeless perfume of cosmic rock and stars. When it loses
the forest, the broken structure of silt and clay washes away
in one mere human lifetime. Interplanetary, hospitable, willing—
if only we were too—hundreds of millions of acres
of horizon—dirt—deep or shallow—could
store our poison and alchemize it into layers of lime
that support themselves, and us, before we are dust that flies, falls,
surrenders and finally gives ourselves away.

Alice B Fogel was New Hampshire poet laureate from 2014 through 2019. She is the author of 5 poetry collections, including *A Doubtful House*; *Interval: Poems Based on Bach's "Goldberg Variations"* which won the Nicholas Schaffner Award for Music in Literature and the New Hampshire Literary Award; and *Be That Empty*, a national bestseller. Another poetry book, *Nothing But*, inspired by Abstract Expressionist art, is forthcoming in fall of 2021, and she is also the author of *Strange Terrain,* a guide to appreciating poetry without necessarily "getting" it. As poet laureate, Alice ran a number of programs, worked with immigrants and refugees, edited an anthology of NH poets' writings, and initiated a youth poet laureate position. Among other awards, Alice has been given a fellowship from the National Endowment for the Arts and a residency at the Carl Sandburg National Historic Site, and her poems have appeared in many journals and anthologies, including *Best American Poetry* and *Best of the Web*. Based in Walpole, NH, she teaches reading and writing workshops in a wide range of areas, works one-on-one with students with learning differences at Landmark College, and hikes mountains whenever possible.

Rich Follett

__Poet Laureate of Strasburg, Virginia__

Sonnet I

From time to time, 'tis human to reflect
On years gone by, and which we might relive,
Sweet reminiscence, pure and circumspect
Entreats of Time what Time will never give:
But when I contemplate the years we've shared,
There's not one treasured hour I would repeat,
Each moment is a perfect jewel most rare,
Without which life could never be replete:
Imagined riches gained by cheating age
Would pale, compared to these—our golden years—
Our loving book, embossed on every page
With wrinkles, silver'd hair, and conquered fears:
Seen thus, remembered youth a folly seems—
Tomorrows spent with you are all my dreams.

Generations

My grandfather was born in gaslight,
Forged boyhood dreams on the Wright Brothers' flight,
Flew a Sopwith Camel in World War I,
Graduated from Princeton under incandescent lights,
And died a wealthy man three weeks shy of his one-hundred-and-first birth-day,
Having wisely invested in a startup company called International Business Machines
Some thirty years before.

My father was born at the start of The Great Depression,
Watched in awe-turned-to-horror as the Hindenburg fell from the sky in flames,
Listened in disbelief to reports of Hiroshima and Nagasaki
On a crystal radio he built from a kit as a boy
(he saved and mailed box tops to claim the treasure),
Lived for a chance to tell the story of talking his mother-in-law into buying a color TV
When she was convinced that it would cause her to go blind,
Taught himself to write code to customize his desktop Dell,
Marveled at the world-wide web,
And kept his beloved flip-phone close at hand
Long after the rest of the world had gone digital.

In the third grade, I went on a field trip with my classmates
To a local airport control tower, where we watched the controllers at work.
Later, we were led to the basement, where we saw twelve enormous blue boxes.
We had to wear earphones to protect ourselves from the roar and
The room was kept at a constant fifty-five degrees
To keep the supercomputers from overheating.

Today I own an iPhone, roughly three inches by four,
Which exceeds by five the capacity
Of those twelve childhood blue monoliths taken together.
Today, I teach adolescents who have never known a day of life without
Personal digital technology in the palm of their hand.

Scientists have determined that the human eyeball
Grows slightly larger with each successive generation.
Humans will have eyes the size of golf balls
One hundred thousand years from now!
That, I will never see, but still I am amazed:
at the crossroads of technology and anatomy,
We are evolving every time we check our e-mail.

Darwin meets the Digital Age—
Hologram at eleven.

Rich Follett is the Poet Laureate of Strasburg, VA. He has published four collections of poetry: *Responsorials* (2009), *Silence, Inhabited* (2011), and *Human &c.* (2013) through NeoPoesis Press, and an ekphrastic collection, *Photo-Ku* (2016) through NightWing Publications. Rich is featured in the Virginia Poets Database through ODU at
https://digitalcommons.odu.edu/virginiapoets.

Chad Frame

Montgomery County, Pennsylvania, Poet Laureate Emeritus

Feeding My Father Pudding While Watching *Bonanza*

All any relationship boils down to
is *are you willing to do this for me*
or aren't you? Hoss and tapioca

and what remains of your life all balanced
precariously on a plastic spoon.
Every week, the grown Cartwright boys learn

another life lesson from their father
who has *seen some things* in his day, who knows
better. And maybe all death really is

is gradual unlearning, the pudding
crusting in your beard like infant spit-up.
I have driven two hundred miles each day

for two weeks to be here to watch old shows,
nurses prodding, your chest rising, falling,
but these are the distances that matter—

spoon to mouth, screen to face, son to father,
father to grave. Your thousand-yard stare's fixed
vaguely on the wall-arm television

where Michael Landon is falling in love
with Bonnie Bedelia, and we know
(half-century old spoiler) that Hoss dies

offscreen because Dan Blocker dies offscreen
from botched surgery. But it is enough
to know the twangy theme is still playing,

galloping into and out of the room,
even when the spoon scrapes an empty cup,
even when we pull the sheets all the way up.

Ghost in the Machine

Six months after you're gone, I'm out driving
your red pickup to your house—both mine, now.

I feel butch in this, raised up and revving
the V6 in this fortress of old smoke,

your ratty, zigzag Mexican blanket
draped over the seats, resin sea turtle

staring wide-eyed from its perch on the dash,
brown dreamcatcher swinging from the rearview.

I'm thankful to be on country backroads
when the truck trundles to ten miles an hour

down from forty and won't speed up again
no matter how hard I stomp the pedal.

Two frustrating miles of this, hazard lights
clicking, my arm out the window waving

cars around—then all at once it speeds up
and I'm squealing sixty around a curve

with no warning and the brakes won't listen
and the horn's blaring and cows flicker by

in quick chiaroscuro and the trees
are just green streaks and the brakes still won't *work*

and then I stop, quickly.   Or almost stop,

back to my ten-mile handicap, inching

forward, and then the speed pattern repeats
in sequence—faster, slower, faster still.

I don't believe in ghosts, yet I still shout
Stop it, dad, my eyes wide, my knuckles white

on the sticky wheel. Somehow, I make it
to a dealership and lurch to a halt,

toss the bewildered valet boy the keys,
muttering *I don't know what the hell's wrong,*

but figure it out.   I'm across the street,
fork scraping a figure eight in egg yolk

on a scratched Denny's plate when my phone rings.
This is weird, a rough voice, no preamble.

It's the mechanic. *You ready for this?*
I answer, *Ready as I'm going to be.*

Back in the shop, he shows me a photo
on his phone—a mouse lodged in the throttle.

He's dead and wadded up, a dried hairball
lodged in an aluminum ring, black streak

down his white back where the engine scorched him.
So, when it sped up or slowed down…? I prompt.

Yes, he says. *That was the mouse opening*

the throttle. You're lucky to be alive,

You're telling me, I ask him, *that this mouse*
was driving my car? He laughs, the harsh grind

of a worn-out clutch. *Pretty much,* he says.
He shares the photo, an urban legend

in the making. *Get a load of this shit,*
other mechanics say. *What are the odds?*

Starting the truck, I think of a photo
I remember someone sharing online

of a dead pike lodged in a tree, small birds
nesting in its jaws. All we need in life

is a safe place to gnaw our way into,
to curl up for warmth. We're only one chomp,

one burning engine, one telephone pole
away from dying at any moment.

What does it say about me, I wonder,
that I would rather believe in your ghost?

Feeding My Father Pudding While Watching Bonanza was originally published in *Philadelphia Stories.*

Ghost in the Machine was originally published in *Schuylkill Valley Journal.*

Chad Frame's work appears in *Rattle, Pedestal, Rust+Moth, Barrelhouse,* and in other journals and anthologies, as well as on iTunes from the Library of Congress. He is the Director of the Montgomery County Poet Laureate Program and a Poet Laureate Emeritus of Montgomery County, Pennsylvania, the Poetry Editor of *Ovunque Siamo: New Italian-American Writing,* a founding member of the No River Twice poetry improv and performance troupe, and the founder of the Caesura Poetry Festival and Retreat. His collection, *Little Black Book,* is forthcoming in 2022 from Finishing Line Press.

Michael S. Glaser

Maryland Poet Laureate, 2004-2009

In the Hospital
(5 years old)

I didn't want her to stick me
and I was going to tell her

she couldn't give me that shot
unless she'd put my toy train

back together again
so that I could pretend

it was taking me away.

But she approached briskly,
told me to roll over

pulled down my bottoms
stuck me and left.

I didn't even whimper. I was too sad,
thinking about my train

and how I didn't know a way
to insist on myself in the world

didn't even know I could.

Elemental Things

"The world today is sick to its thin blood
for elemental things."

. . . *Henry Beston*

Gridlocked on the freeway, what I know
is the future framed in a window
that looks out at a sea of concrete
and dangerous machines.

I move from here to there and back again,
commute long distances, listen to the news,
music, talk radio. I become impatient,
angry, do foolish things

curse my fellow travelers
commuting like me back and forth,
back and forth
week after week after week.

If someone were to knock on my door
and invite me into elemental things –
earth, air, fire before the hands
water welling from the earth--

what would I answer?
How would I know to respond?

Michael S. Glaser is a Professor Emeritus at St. Mary's College of Maryland and served as Poet Laureate of Maryland from 2004-2009. The recipient of the Homer Dodge Endowed Award for Excellence in Teaching, the Columbia Merit Award for service to poetry, Loyola College's Andrew White Medal for contributions to the intellectual and artistic life in Maryland, he recently completed two terms as a member of the Board of Directors of the Maryland Humanities Council. Glaser has edited three anthologies of poetry, co-edited the Complete Poems of Lucille Clifton for BOA Editions, and published several award winning volumes of his own work, most recently Threshold of Light with Bright Hill Publishing (2019). More at www.michaelsglaser.com

Bill Glose

Daily Press Poet Laureate, 2011

Harbinger

On the welcome mat
outside Dawn's back door,

her cat has been leaving gifts,
Carolina wrens with broken necks,

moles with velvet fur
and star-shaped noses,

now limp as a failed notion.
She wonders what it means.

All I can offer is knowledge—
my belief in science and formulas,

probabilities and statistics,
tensile strengths of materials.

I can appreciate the beauty
of a bell curve and the likelihood

of multiple outcomes, skills
as unhelpful as unwanted.

So I hold the ladder in Dawn's foyer
as she climbs its rubberized steps

to water plants on the ledge, their vines
trailing down the faux brick façade,

my hands on her calves as I look up,
hoping she won't fall.

Dark Matter

Nights when black swallows the moon,
gulps down crescent-bit remainders
reflecting another continent's sun,

emptiness of space yawns into lungs
like comets cresting event horizons,
streaking tails stretching as they slip

into black holes. Copernicus once spurned
religious doctrine to proclaim Earth
spun round the sun, not the other way around.

Now he ponders whether dark matter exists,
an all-encompassing power
impossible to scoop up and study in a lab.

A kind of faith, the way minds fill in
what eyes can't see or hands grasp.
The heart believing that invisible energy

rules our world, spins its axis,
pushes its orbit round a star
we hope will rise again tomorrow.

A former paratrooper and combat veteran, Bill Glose writes poetry for catharsis and to pick at the many things he doesn't understand. His current work reflects upon the dread-filled months after his girlfriend was diagnosed with terminal lung cancer and the stunned relief when her tumor shrank and disappeared. The author of five poetry collections and hundreds of magazine articles, Glose was named the *Daily Press* Poet Laureate in 2011 and featured by NPR on *The Writer's Almanac* in 2017. His poems have appeared in numerous journals, including *Rattle*, *Poet Lore*, *Narrative Magazine*, and *The Sun*. He maintains a page of helpful information for writers on his website at www.billglose.com.

Gabor G Gyukics

__Lifetime Beat Poet Laureate, Hungary__

creating your own music

the early troglodytes might have dispised the shindig of birds
especially the cawing of crows
to beguile the tedium of watching a blunt pointed angle
they chopped wood after wood to pieces
chased thousands of mantis and cockroach from the greens of their caves
tried avoiding to hear the footfall of ghosts
by entering someone elses's thoughts
parted the meadow covered with fiddlehead ferns
the surface of their long built path across the hills
which was shaped by roots of every tree they had known
around the crevasses of earth
emitting particles of previously inhaled fog of density
when the thunders slept
they decorated long narrow sticks with tales heard from wild horses
carved violins out of split wood
glued the pieces together with resin
used the intestines of a fallen once hungrywolf for strings
lifted all to their shoulders
and began to play

volumetric analysis

the perfect pronunciation may seem unnatural
in this ostensibly reprimanded formless morning cavalcade
turning into a shapeless day of an akward evening
lost in a mute doorframe
leading to a a private cloud of a colorful sky
full with goshawks calling each other
pointing out the plummeting temperature
in the surrounding cities where people
live off the grid due to introvert
blindsided authorities ostentatiously lurking around
protected by their frozen shells
without explicable reason that would make them
taintless before the spirits
and their invented gods
with thin-lipped smiles

Gabor G Gyukics, Budapest born poet, translator, author of 11 books of poetry in five languages, 1 book of prose and 16 books of translations including *A Transparent Lion*, selected poetry of Attila József, ***They'll Be Good for Seed,*** an anthology of contemporary Hungarian poetry in English and an anthology of North American Indigenous poets in Hungarian titled ***Medvefelhő a város felett***. He's writing poetry in English and Hungarian.

Alexandra "Zan" Delaine Hailey

Prince William County, Virginia, Poet Laureate 2014-2016

Around the Yellow House

The train passes—a heavy
heart—beating down the tracks.

A U-turning rickety pick-up,
matte black finish—brings dogs
to a bark across the block.

Afternoon planes fly—streaking contrails,
connecting cumulonimbus clouds.

A letter from an uncensored inmate
was left in my mailbox while I was out
walking a fuchsia petaled path,

where wild Dogwoods fade pink
with the gold of magnolias,

leaving a perfume alley trail.
A squirrel bats its tail like a duster
on a bookshelf—take in the day.

Open it slow—pocketknife blade
soundly tearing a slit—*Dear Wonderful.*

Previously published in *The Northern Virginia Review: Volume No. 33-Spring 2019.*

Vincent, *Out of Doors*
          —Looking at *Bedroom in Arles*—

Away from Paris, farther south,
the sun beats stronger tangerine
strokes on white lilac—scoring
colours of the prism, veiled

in mist; before western skies
flower red. *I take revenge*
on my bedroom with tilted brushes.
A wicker-backed chair, unsittable

against the closed door embedded
in royal washed plaster, facing
its wooden partner, who sits patiently
beneath an out-bent window,

lit by Number Two Chrome
that brightens a small collection
of polished sketches—bowed copper
wire, dangling silhouettes—above

my periscoped bed frame, where
sleep fractures vibrant oils
on blank canvas. Think, more
Japanese. *A single blade*

of grass; verdant concave, veins
scaffolding a rooted spine. *Simple*
as buttoning your waistcoat.
Rays horizontal blue

brazing cobblestone streets,
where violet figures pattern *a host*
of new subjects—night prowlers—
with indigo strolling shadows.

Italicized words borrowed from Vincent Van Gogh's letters written to his
brother Theo.

Alexandra "Zan" Delaine Hailey was an inaugural poet laureate in Prince
William County, VA, 2014-2016. Her poetry and nonfiction have been pub-
lished in *The Northern Virginia Review, Written in Arlington, Prince William
Living*, Virginia Commonwealth University's Focused Inquiry Textbook,
Bristow Beat, and *New Departures: Write By The Rails Anthology*. Poetry is
forthcoming in *The Poetry Society of Virginia Centennial Anthology* and in
her chapbook, *Intrastate Lines*.

Debra Hall

Racine, Wisconsin, Poet Laureate

Flight Risk

I am a foreigner
suspended at the terminal
sent back to the embassy.
To exchange all that I own
at the turnstile
to meet my agent.
I count the holes that penetrate
the glass between us
try to pull her words through
ask her to repeat what she said
it will be awhile
until you are free to leave this country.
I am far from home
the man on the corner sees my fear
leers at me
the man behind me
at the deli
asks for money
He pinches my sleeve
behind loaves of bread
gestures his hand to mouth
per favore, vorrei mangiare
"please, I want to eat"
I linger at the meat counter

The butcher tells the man
lasciala da sola "leave her alone".
I recount euros
then raise my eyes to the urgent man
let him know
I will keep what's mine.

Un terremoto - An earthquake

I touched down
in a village
high in the mountains
of Costa Rica
a place to remarry
ears and tongue
with a second
language.
My cheeks blushed
when my host family told jokes.
I stumbled to catch
the punch line
and laughed too late.
My sister gave me
the joke book so I
could follow along.

Late at night an earthquake
shook the house.
My sister said
it was just a temblor,
an aftershock from a bigger quake
in Panama
el primero respiro de un niño tan genial como un terremoto
"the first breath of a child as awesome as an earthquake"
My sister said
ten years ago
a bigger quake hit the village.
Part of the mountain
came down like a
dull, heavy knife

on people and animals
asleep in houses and fields

After breakfast we walked
to the place where
the rock touched down
a mile from the house.
The rock now a leg
bent at the knee
like a large child skiing
down the mountain.

We drove to a cloud forest
with air as thin as thread.
As we stood on the edge
of a soft white sea,
my sister said this was where the
earthquake split the mother from her child
for the breath of the village below...
 el primero respiro de un niño tan genial como un terremoto.

Debra Hall, a Wisconsin native who loves Romance languages, international travel and close proximity to Lake Michigan. During the school year, she is a high school Spanish teacher and during summer, she practices beach yoga with her dog, Salma. Her poems have been published in anthologies and magazines. She is currently working on a chapbook on resilience. She is the current Poet Laureate of Racine, Wisconsin.

Hazel Clayton Harrison

Altadena Public Library, California, Poet Laureate, 2018-2020

Love Letter To My Dad

Dear Dad,

From the day I was born, you were my steady rock, my mighty oak, my shining star. I remember how you used to carry me on your shoulders, and bounce me on your knee. Though you were tired after working all day at the mill, you'd climb the stairs
at night to tell me a bedtime story.

Watching you get down on your knees at night, I learned how to pray.
When I became a rebellious teenager and your rules I refused to obey
you lectured me, but never gave up hope. I guess you knew that sooner or later
I'd come to my senses. You'd always send me a check when I went away to school
and needed help paying my college expenses.

I'll never forget the day your doctor delivered the sad news. He said you had only months to live. Unable to bear that thought of you leaving me behind, I cried my eyes out. But on your journey through the valley
you taught me how to face death with humility, grace, and dignity.

You're gone now, but not a single day goes by that I don't thank God for giving me you as a father. I'm still trying to follow in your footsteps. Sometimes I stumble and fall, but I still feel your hand reaching down to lift me up. I love you Dad.

And in my heart you'll always be my steady rock, my mighty oak, my shining star.

Bird Watching

Have you noticed lately that not even birds
congregate on phone wires anymore?

Remember how they used to flock together
singing their wild love songs?

Now they perch in pairs standing feet a part
It's been months since we were told to stay

inside and distance ourselves when taking walks
The last time I saw my daughter I wanted to hug

her so badly. With tears in my eyes, I watched her
walk away

No one knows when the quarantine will end
No one knows when we'll be able to congregate
in churches and schools

Or dance holding hands. In the meantime
I'll look to the skies, keeping my eyes on the birds.

Hazel Clayton Harrison served as Poet Laureate, Community Events 2018-2020 for the Altadena Public Library. Her poetry has been widely anthologized in literary journals, including the *When the Virus Came Calling, Altadena Literary Review* 2020, *Coiled Serpent, Grandfathers,* and *A Rock Against the Wind.* She is the author of, *Down Freedom Road,* a collection of poetry and prose, and a memoir, *Crossing the River Ohio.* Her books are available at jahlightmedia.com, shabdapress.com and Amazon.

Bill Hayden

Norwalk, Connecticut, Poet Laureate 2019

Ferry Crossing

Fog lapse grin throb
put rich tones in store
(I hear)
Relentless motor needing
Passage to wild steel acres of the gods'
Own making music to the motor-laden ears
(as if)
Our voices needed underlines
Of rotten churning pistons, so that
An aging, flexible box of voice, could
(deaf to its owner's ears)
Reveal the tortuous trail that took it over,
Confess to the chains its owner's body wore
And count the weight of every suffered link
That kept him near forgiving motor needs
Precisely where the engine calls for oil,
See how he forces out the gun
Its sacred petrol tears
See the thanks he's giving now
To beautiful gears

Bill Hayden grew up on a fresh water lake in Northern Westchester County, New York and developed a love for and a rapport with nature while stretching his imagination and experiencing a feeling of being connected with the natural world. He started writing poems in his teenage years and pursued it some during college, but it wasn't until attending some poetry workshops in the Fairfield County, Connecticut area near his home in Norwalk that he began writing more regularly. He was the assistant editor of The Little Apple, a literary and arts magazine based in Norwalk, working along with fellow poet and editor Henry Lyman, they produced four issues over a 2 year period in the early 1980's. In April of 2019, Bill was selected to become Norwalk's 2nd Poet Laureate, following in the footsteps of Laurel Peterson, who held the position for 3 years. His twice-monthly Norwalk Poetry Workshop has been held since June 2019, first at the main branch of the Norwalk Public Library, and lately on Zoom since the pandemic hit. The group of poets have taken part in a couple of ekphrastic poetry writing workshops held at local art galleries, and members of the group have been featured on the online Poetry Page of the library. Bill has had a couple of his poems published in local anthologies in the past couple of years, and hopes to be able to host poetry readings in the future, featuring published poets from around the region.

Sam Hazo

Pennsylvania Poet Laureate, Emeritus

No Option But One

Whatever could have been
or still might be comes
without warning in our sleep.
The days of pain that never
happened happen.
Dreams
of bounty or misjudgment differ
only in degree and outcome
from nausea to guilt.
Excess
breeds regret.
Soldiers
rise legless or armless or both
from ranks of identical graves,
accusing, accusing, accusing.
We struggle not to listen.
Titles like Mr. President,
Your Royal Highness,
You Holiness, Your Honor,
Your Grace or anyone who holds
the office of citizen mean nothing.
The bitter truth of nightmares

comes without our wiling it.
Waking wiser or spared,
our last defense is gratitude.

The author of books of poetry, fiction, essays and plays, Samuel Hazo is the founder and director of the International Poetry Forum in Pittsburgh, Pennsylvania. He is also McAnulty Distinguished Professor of English Emeritus at Duquesne University, where he taught for forty-three years. From 1950 until 1957 he served in the United States Marine Corps, completing his tour as a captain. He earned his Bachelor of Arts degree *magna cum laude* from the University of Notre Dame, a Master of Arts degree from Duquesne University and his doctorate from the University of Pittsburgh.

Gladys Henderson

Poet Laureate of Suffolk County 2017-2019

Memorial Day at Short Beach

1.

Sun shakes its stars on the Nissequogue, a lone kayaker
paddles against its current; the drop tide carries everything
with it that does not resist. Marsh flats exposed appear
as main lands of some foreign shore. Gulls fish their umber
skins, the work easier now, that spring has arrived.

The kayaker has decided to surrender, his ample arms not strong
enough to go against the tide. The river plays with his intent, but
in time he glides in front of me, making swift his way towards shore.

This morning a child's face on the news returns to haunt me,
he screams in his father's arms as they race out of their village.

2.

Above the light fixture an osprey nest, parents tending a hungry
chick. Devoted guardians, I watch as they plunge into the currents,
bodies under water, lungs without air, and rise up from the cobalt ribbon
like Lazarus, talons clenching their offspring's meal.

There were no other faces, only backs, legs, shoulders of stampeding humans, death mushrooms rising from the horizon, hysteria carrying all of them. No mother, perhaps she was ahead of them or maybe dead. His arms reached out; they reached out for me to save him.

Mourning Dove

She struggled off her legs, only to sit down again.
Eyes closed, nodding off, mid afternoon,
she wanted to sleep, to rest her head beneath
her wing. He looked down at her, fluffed his neck,
cooed his love, circled her sleeping body
but she would not move. I rose from my rocker,
left my voyeur's seat. Startled, the male flew
into the pines, watched as I touched the female
with my finger. I was God touching Adam,
but I felt death in the stillness of her body, not life.

I returned to my chair not wanting to believe
she was dead. The male rushed back to her side,
began to preen her head. Around her still body
he cooed and danced, feathers iridescent
in the afternoon sun; his throat fluffed with air.
I wanted it to be over, his attention to her so tender,
painful for me to watch. I brought out my shovel
from the shed, a plastic bag to guard my hand,
and dug her grave. I saw him watch as I picked
her up and placed her into the hole, covering
her with earth. From out of the pines, the male
flew to the loose soil above her grave. In gestures
both foreign and familiar, he began to coo and dance
above her body. Throat feathers extended from
his song breath, beak pecking the earth in a frantic
heat, he looked up at me as if to say,
What have you done? Where have you taken her?

Having no answers, I spoke to him about you.
How still you lay in your coffin, the painted rose
on your cheeks making you look alive. How I touched
your hand before they closed the lid, how I watched
the doves in the trees while they shoveled dirt
on your body, the sound unbearable to my ears,
the vision of your covered face too agonizing.
He circled the ground above her once more
and with one long coooo, escaped into the late afternoon
haze, the stillness of the air trembling with death.

Gladys Henderson's poems are widely published and have been featured on PBS Channel 21 in their production, *Shoreline Sonata*. Her work has appeared in several journals and anthologies including: *A Taste of Poetry, Avocet, Bard's Annual, Block Island Poetry Project, For Loving Precious Beast, Great Neck Plaza Public Poetry Project, Kaleidoscope, Long Island Sounds, Long Island Quarterly, Mason's Road, Oberon, Paumanok, Paumanok: Performance Poets Association Literary Review, Interwoven, Poetry Bay, Presence, Primal Sanities, Songs of Seasoned Women, String Poetry Journal, Suffolk County Poetry Review, The Light of City and Sea, Towards Forgiveness, Whispers and Shouts, Xanadu*, as well as many other publications. She was co-editor of the anthology *Leaves of me…*published by Early Lilacs Press, 2019. Nationally she was a finalist for the Paumanok Poetry Prize 2006, has received recognition in the Writer's Digest Poetry Competitions 2008, 2009, 2012. Finishing Line Press published her chapbook, *Eclipse of Heaven* in 2009. She was named the Walt Whitman Birthplace Poet of the Year in 2010, and was chosen Poet Laureate of Suffolk County 2017-2019.

Ngoma Hill

__Beat Poet Laureate, New York State, 2017-2019__

Pestilence

This aint the first pestilence
the Holy Babble even gave warning
it may not be the last
it's another chapter
payment of karmic debt
a time to look at all the history
you want me to forget
but the statues of Confederacy
are still standing on my chest
and the knee of killer kops
remain on my neck
and I'm trying to figure out
why we ain't figured out
that we're standing at the
cross road
at the intersection of Corona Blvd,Gun Ave
and Killa Kops
so tell Becky don't throw a Karen
the pimple of poverty is about to burst
and it's gonna take more than skin cream
this acne been building
since the "Good Ship Jesus"
everything is everything
and all things are connected

seems like the septic tank of life
is backed up
while the resident in the white's house
continues to play golf
in some altered state of reality
blind to the fact that
the truth in bold yellow letters
has been painted on the Ave
of his Luxury Bldg
telling the whole damned world that
"Black Lives Matter"

Ngoma is a performance poet,multi -instrumentalist,singer / song-writer,Artivist and paradigm shifter, who for over 50 years has used culture as a tool to raise socio-political and spiritual consciousness through work that encourages critical thought. A former member of Amiri Baraka's "The Spirit House Movers and Players" and the contemporary freedom song duo "Serious Bizness",Ngoma weaves poetry and song that raises contradictions and searches for a solution to a just and peaceful world. Ngoma was the Prop Slam Winner of the 1997 National Poetry Slam Competition in Middletown,CT and has been published in African Voices Magazine,Long Shot Anthology,The Underwood Review,Signifyin' Harlem Review,Bum Rush the Page/Def Poetry Jam Anthology,Poems on the Road to Peace-(Volumes 1,2,and 3)Yale Press and Let Loose On the World-Amiri Baraka at 75. The Understanding Between Foxes and Light-Great Weather For Media and New Rain/Blind Beggar Press 35th Anniversary Issue. He was featured in the P.B.S spoken word documentary The Apropoets with Allen Ginsburg Ngoma was selected as the Beat Poet Laureate of New York for 2017 by The National Beat Poetry Poetry Foundatio.n

Joan Hoffman

Poet Laureate of Canton, Connecticut

Good Morning

Loosely knotted our bodies recline within each other
and I feel your spine, not stiff like your voice

when you reprimanded yourself for forgetting
to close the door to the hen house, rather soft

like peach as I thumbed up and down to unleash
a trigger of muscle from a firmness of flesh recumbent

while you absorb each press's insistence that you give up
whatever resistance you hold dear. All living things

breathe in one form or another. Your concave goes with
my convex against the angle of hip. Bone carved into

the mattress after so many years, the vine of your leg,
shoulder resting against my breast while I tongue your lobe

you whimper gently, widen your neck for pleasure, lift
your chin before you thrust it into my chest your palms

cradling my cheeks nostrils to nostrils to breath the luxury
of warmness, a vault of heaven's affection in a morning

harvest, delicate eggs newly hardened from roosting hens.

Joan Hofmann, Professor Emerita at the University of Saint Joseph, serves on
the Riverwood Poetry Board, and was the inaugural Poet Laureate of Canton,
CT. Author of three chapbooks: Coming Back, Alive, and Alive, Too, her
poems are published or forthcoming in anthologies and journals, including:
Forgotten Women, Waking Up to the Earth, Concho River Review, Tiger
Moth Review, Wild Word, Connecticut River Review, Buddhist Poetry Re-
view, Bird's Thumb, The Wayfarer, Dillydoun Review, Canary, SLANT, and
Plainsongs.

Larry Jaffe

__Florida Beat Poet Laureate__

Running The Human Race

Running the human race
is like seeking god
at a hotdog stand
when not every stand
has a good dog

Running the human race
is like being on a treadmill
to nowhere
and where you are
is nowhere you wanted to be

I stopped running the human race

I stopped running the human race
it was too much like competition
and relationships became estranged
scattered to the elements
friends became enemies
and enemies stayed that way

I stopped running the human race
and went for a walk on the wild side
gesturing to Lou Reed
he gave me a silent wave

and secret handshake
I knew it was the right thing to do

I stopped running the human race
because it was stunting my growth
and caused my creativity to cancel itself
I had been broadcasting senility
and disingenuity was becoming my brainchild
I could not write if I could not be at peace

I stopped running the human race
and went to a place where
we did not vote for governors
we governed ourselves
gender was irrelevant
and color only added to the beauty

Ars Poetica

She found the crucible
of broken fate
a divine aesthetic
of ribboned notes

From the rubbish
she formed
a musical seascape
a symphony of color
a tapestry of sound

I beseech you
to call my name
in poetry
speak to me in verse
allow me entrance
to the sculpture

For his entire professional career, Larry Jaffe has been using his art to promote human rights. He was Poet-In-Residence at the Autry Museum of Western Heritage, a featured poet in Chrysler's Spirit in the Words poetry program, co-founder of Poets for Peace (now Poets without Borders), helped spearhead the United Nations Dialogue among Civilizations through Poetry project with hundreds of readings globally using the aesthetic power of poetry to bring understanding to the world, former Poet Laureate Youth for Human Rights and the Florida Beat Poet Laureate. He was the recipient of the Saint Hill Art Festival's Lifetime of Creativity Award. . He has six books of poetry: *Unprotected Poetry, Anguish of the Blacksmith's Forge, One Child Sold, In Plain View, 30 Aught 4, Sirens* and *Man without Borders*.

Doc Janning

South Euclid, Ohio, Poet Laureate

A Thousand Billion Stars

Evening softly draws
 Sun into dusk
(ghost of the day)
as secret voice
of infinite night
calls in eldritch tones
through warrens of time
and darkness rushes
on fey silent wings
infusing magick
into echoing cavern
of ageless black sky
melding and blending
with lambent shine
of a thousand billion stars.

"Doc" Janning, the 77-year-old Inaugural Poet Laureate of South Euclid, Ohio, is a poet, author, educator, longtime Scout Leader, and retired Podiatrist. He has created Ekphrastic Poetry for Heights Arts in Cleveland Heights, OH, and for Cleveland Photo Fest. He has been a Writer-in-the-Window at Appletree Books for National Novel Writers' Month. He is Creator-Moderator of Second Sunday Poets, a poetry open mic sponsored by the William N. Skirball Writers' Center at the South Euclid - Lyndhurst Branch of the Cuyahoga County Public Library, which has published some of his work, and Creator-Moderator of Awenites, a biweekly online poetry event. One of his poems has also been published in Lyndhurst (OH) Life Magazine for June 2020, another appears on PoemHunter.com, and a recent piece is to appear in an anthology to be published by the Wick Poetry Center of Kent State University (OH).

Chuck Joy

**Erie County, Pennsylvania, Poet Laureate 2018-2020**

Pine Hill Summit

Pennsylvania's filled with clouds today
only the highest elevations have escaped them

Where we are, and the air is clear
warm for this time of year

The mountains are red with the October forest
hillsides mad hides to make an impossible suede

When we turn down the music in the dashboard
our words turn into poetry before we speak them

       *   *   *

At a trailhead near a railroad bridge
we park and leave our car forever

Abandoning our families and their dreams
our exercise routines and every other thing

The path is soft with moss and not too steep
it climbs beside a black and rocky creek

144

Until we reach the meadow at the top
where the bear and the deer are, and the hawk

And a cabin with firewood stacked next to it
where we could choose to live

The Minarets of Erie

talking keeps us together
framing specific configurations of sound with tongue and lips
words, the process well-polished, just below consciousness
it's a trip

no trumpet between us and it
no reed or row of metal holes
just muscles and spit and spirit, an intention
then voice, clear and sweet or hoarse or sharp

*   *   *

always talking, always in English
occasional accents in pidgin Spanish
rarely that schtick of pretend German gibberish
achtgemeinerleiberfrunkenmitcha dankeshoen

language phrased with wit
powerful medicine, balm to the ills that plague us
me at least, the fever of anger, the chills of despair
heart failure, all the pathologies
every affliction, traumatic accident, anxiety, addiction
every perturbation of consciousness threatening us, dimming our vision

the source of life, breath
the sum of all philosophy all religion, breathing
breath brings us meaning
and next to breathing, speech

The Minarets of Erie, is published under the title Speaking Words in Vol. XVII, No. 4, Winter 2021-22 in Pratik, A Magazine of Contemporary Writing from Nepal.

Chuck Joy, Poet Laureate Erie County Pennsylvania 2018-2020. Author, *Said the Growling Dog, Percussive, Fun Poetry, Theme of Line, Every Tiger Wants To Sing*. Recent magazines: *Red Fez, Pratik*. Host, Poetry Night. Member, Italian-American Writers Association. Child and Adolescent Psychiatrist (University of Pittsburgh School of Medicine 1978).

Evelyn Kandel

Nassau County, New York Poet Laureate 2019-2022

Thoughts On Being Poet Laureate During a Pandemic.

Poet Laureate, an honor practically no one except poets
care about; no one knows what it is or who you are, don't know
that Ancient Greeks and Romans picked leaves of a Laurel tree
to weave them around heads of poets proclaiming their fame.

Background stories like that aren't exactly on the current
best-seller list or on the web that everyone knows and *likes*.
So where does being poet laureate leave me in the popularity
contest? Will what I have written live on in literary journals?

Perhaps not, but I am proud to explain it all to puzzled people.
Writing my poems gives me pleasure, having them published too.
I like introducing myself as laureate and reading my poems aloud.
So I bid *adieu* and wave *good-by* with a little smile of satisfaction.

How It Is Now

There is turbulence in the river now
Where once the stream flowed slowly

You have slipped away my dear
    You have gone away

This river we call life is flowing
    As you slipped away, my own

I am standing here on the dock
    Watching alone

You are on a ship on this mighty river
    Sailing away

I am here on the shore
    Destined to stay

And all the clever rhymes
    Or lovely phrases

Do not alter this leaving
    Or make more bearable

How it is now.

Evelyn Kandel was Nassau County Poet Laureate, 2019-22. She teaches poetry classes to adults at Great Neck Community Center, Glen Cove Library, LIU's Hutton House and this fall will teach her zoom class privately. Author of 5 books of poetry, her latest **Let There Be Clouds** contains poems illustrated by her own sky photos. Her recent poems are in **Corona** edited by Gayl Teller and **Paumonauk, Transitions** edited by Kathy Donnelly. She is also a proud Marine Corps veteran.

Wendi R. Kaplan

Alexandria, Virginia, Poet Laureate, 2016-2019

Knowing

You were ten
          and knew
somehow.
The principal called,
asked me to join you
in her office,
as you were not speaking.

I entered and saw you slouched,
planted in the big chair,
your blonde bangs hiding your eyes...
"What's going on?" I ask gently and
you begin to cry,
tears and words cascade,
bursting through your carefully placed dam...
"Keanu got in trouble for talking
and teacher sent him to the principal, but I
was talking too and she didn't send me
because I have blue eyes; she sent Keanu
because he is dark black and...and
it's not fair."

My tears and the principal's tears
have joined yours.

I kneel in front of you,
take your hands,
"You did the right thing son,
you did the right thing."

You knew.
And you, a boy of few words,
a friend of silence,
an observer of the world,

You knew.
And reminded us
that we know.
We do.

To observe is to learn,
is to know,
and, if we can,
to do.

To Poets Every One

To all of the poets,
each one of you
willing to look lovingly, boldly,
at the moments of the day,
the landscapes of our lives,
as well as the dust
in the eyes of the child
after the bombs pour down,
at the leathered bark of the
elephants' skin,
at the brilliant blue
of the startled blue jay
that has visited the lilac bush.

To all of you,
poets every one —
willing to listen
to the November wind
and the crumple of falling leaves,
to the hushed quiet of falling
snowflakes,
to the surprise gasps of hope
as violets emerge in early spring,
and to the fiesta music of summer,
alive with zucchini and zinnias
popping in percussive color.

To all of the poets
who teach us to pause,
to observe, to wonder,

to be amazed—
by the miracles
that lay in each drop
of each day,
whether bleak and grey,
whether quiet,
 or a colorful display—
that open us
to the common, yellow onion,
to the peacock proud
bird of paradise,
to the quiver in the dog's nose,
the squirrel on the sunny branch
in quiet repose.

To all of you,
poets every one,
poets,
everyone.

Wendi R. Kaplan was the Poet Laureate of Alexandria Virginia (2016-2019). Her self-defined mission during her term was to Build Bridges and Create Community. She believes that poetry illuminates life and that we are all poets. She knows that poetry can give people a voice, even when they feel they have none. Wendi has been an Alexandria resident and community activist since 1982. She has been writing and reading poetry as long as she can remember. Wendi's poetry reflects her observations of the world, of nature, of people and of the exquisite awareness of the extraordinary in the present moment. Wendi is a clinical social worker and certified poetry therapist. She has taught at The American University and at The George Washington University School of Medicine. She is also a long-time meditator which colors her work and writing. Poetry threads through all of her life.

Tori Lane Kovarik

Alexandria, Virginia, Poet Laureate 2013-2016

Art is Order

Dividing the paved street from the dust and dirt of unfinished road,
there are concrete dividers sitting under the stop light,
perpetually flashing red, which is under the new bridge I like to fly over.
On the concrete dividers, people I'll never meet have doodled with spray cans,
graffiti I cannot decipher save for the one bold statement in black,
articulated clearly, precisely, atop the rest.
Art is Order the black paint unequivocally declares,
the statement mimicked in strength of letter and line.
Art is order to the one who denied the ordering law
and shook the can, maybe danced to created beat,
painted on the concrete under flashing red lights
that separate the paved roads of completion
from the dust and dirt of the yet to be constructed.
Art is order in the way a heart thumps steadily,
until the day it bows out of the ballroom dance,
the day when it refuses to so much as even sway,
moved by rhythmic melody while standing against the wall.
Art is order in the way snow falls,
wavering between flickering flurries and
large white chunks of molting angels wings falling to earth.
Art is order in the way I've known someone for years
and yesterday was the first time I nearly choked on the blue of his eyes.
Art is order in the way red wine sits majestically in a glass
and the way it looks like blood,

155

so blood too must look beautiful in a glass,
swirling out of a bottle into the deathlike stillness of my glass
before being swallowed down to dance with hot, living blood,
the red wine beauty of my veins.
Art is order in the way people pray to an unseen God
but know, they know, they know that unseen divine thing
is more real than any wind turned air they suck into despairing lungs.
Art is order in the way I, preschool teacher, seminary student, dancer, poet,
want to be dressed all in black under the star sprayed sky,
dancing to the created beats of a shaking spray paint can,
making bold statements on concrete,
which is firmer than the paper of notebooks
and all the air I've thrown words upon,
dancing in the red glow of flashing lights
under the new bridge I like to fly over.

The First Nights of Autumn

Snap the spine of the paperback book,
flick the ash from the cigarette,
the sun will dip behind the moon
and give away the evening hours
with a cup of coffee, leather jacket,
and notes tucked into the margins.
The umbrella protects from the falling stars
and collects the smoky breath of poetry
exhaled on the air of change.
This is the time of transformation,
of the alteration of persons,
the reclamation of all beautiful things.
The night is impressionable,
scarred with the memories of its day,
tattooed with hopes for the dark of its mystery
and the dawn it so graciously precedes.
Grief is cradled in the words of her hand,
healing murmured in the lines of constellations,
sought, not always seen,
ever present in the darkened heavens
which dare the smoke to join it
in watching over the transitioning world.
The poet settles in to decipher the graffiti
of the smoke and stars sprayed overhead,
reading of history and God in the grey moon
and the white spaces of broken backed literature.

Tori Lane Kovarik is a poet and visual artist living in northern Virginia. She served as Poet Laureate of the City of Alexandria from 2013-2016. Tori has published two poetry collections, done numerous readings and performances in northern Virginia, as well as shown her visual art in Virginia, Maryland, Vermont, and North Carolina. Tori writes about a wide variety of topics, including teaching, the writing process, community, faith and spiritual crisis, trauma and healing, and motherhood. Her writing is full of colorful observations, brutal honesty, and flashes of whimsy. Tori's aim in writing and performing poetry is to speak the unspeakable, highlight the seemingly mundane, and give voice to the voiceless.

Carolyn Kreiter-Foronda

Poet Laureate of Virginia, 2006-2008

Overlooking the City, I Reminisce

about women in homeless
shelters who have nothing
to do but imagine their fate:
overdose, a gun, a husband
who demands his wife
heed his dicey commands.

In a split second, a woman
begging on a street corner
falls to the pavement.
Epileptic seizures shake
her limbs with the force
of a tempestuous wind.
In flashing streetlights her dark
skin glistens. Her front teeth
tumble onto the sidewalk.
I call out to drivers to dial 9-1-1,
their slapdash haste, egregious.

I tell myself, *Don't dwell
on the madness, the insane
chatter of hurried drivers,
the headstrong haste
of pedestrians.* I pillow

the fallen woman's head
in my lap, place a sweater
beneath her neck, thank
a passerby for calling
an ambulance, a siren's
shrill wail in the distance.

I dwell on this craziness,
on humanity's self-absorption,
wonder why it took over an hour
for someone to seek help,
wonder if the woman will live,
if she'll end up in the shelter
where I read poetry to pregnant
Hope while she clapped, danced,
beat the blues on tin cans,
where Gwendolyn stood tall
and chanted, where a woman
like the one I sought to save
crouched in a corner, extended
her hand, begged for a quarter.

"Overlooking the City, I Reminisce" was published in *Artemis 2020,* Volume
XXVII.

Christmas in Bolivia

On the streets of Cochabamba, Indian women sell miniatures of Mary, Joseph, the three kings. My husband holds up a four-foot pine, bargains the price down, then smiles, boyhood all over his face, good to be home where he can decorate the tree in the native reds, greens, and blues of this fertile pampa. Hot, the streets of this city, close to the sun. I look up at the fabled god *Inti* showering the cathedral, its tower of bells and clock marking the hour: noon, the stone condor aloft its perch in the plaza *Catorce de Septiembre*, mythical bird lifting its wings brought alive by *Inti's* fire and the trick of midday glare.

My husband drops *bolivianos* into the cup of a blind woman seated by the cathedral doors. Her face, furrowed and browned, softens in the protective shadows as if she senses the sparrow skittering toward her. Flapping its wings, it lifts, then touches down on the woman's cup, tipping it over, causing her to jump and grab the tin vessel as if to avoid a robber. My husband leans down and rights the container. Speaking in soothing tones, he pours the coins from the cup into her hands so she can count them, their size and weight familiar to her fingers.

I lower my head and ask for the sparrow to bless this Indian woman. In the square someone plays the *quena* as though he has swallowed the wind.

"Christmas in Bolivia" was originally published in *Hispanic Culture Review* and was reprinted in *The Dead Mule School of Southern Literature* and in the author's books, *Gathering Light* and *These Flecks of Color: New and Selected Poems*.

Carolyn Kreiter-Foronda, Virginia Poet Laureate Emerita, has co-edited four anthologies, co-authored a poem-play, and published nine books of poetry, including *The Embrace: Diego Rivera and Frida Kahlo*, winner of the international Art in Literature: The Mary Lynn Kotz Award. She is the recipient of five grants from the Virginia Commission for the Arts and has won the Ellen Anderson Award, multiple first place awards from the Chesapeake Bay Branch of the National League of American Pen Women, a resolution of appreciation from the Virginia Board of Education for her service as poet laureate, an Edgar Allan Poe Poetry Award, six Pushcart Prize nominations, as well as other awards. Her poems appear in numerous journals and anthologies, including *Nimrod, Prairie Schooner, Mid-American Review, Best of Literary Journals, Poet Lore,* and *World Poetry Yearbook.*
https://www.carolynforonda.com

Jim Landwehr

Village of Wales, Wisconsin, Poet Laureate

July Heat

The cat sees a fly it cannot reach
taunting her from high on the wall
like a mountaineering fly
it rappels down the face of the wall
using its sticky dogshit feet
as the cat stalks it from base camp #2

When the alpine fly takes to the wing
in search of a higher wall or maybe a roadkill
the cat changes her focus to her tail
which she forgets is hers and mistakes
for a threatening, elusive weasel
that has somehow fused to her torso

The alleged owner of the cat
- alleged because the cat's not
all onboard with the idea as yet -
observes like he's watching a
black and white movie in
a smoky theater in Terra Haute

Minutes later the cat has lost interest
in everything but her next nap
she sleeps like the queen of Glasgow

163

oblivious to the pending asteroid shower
and the double rainbow in Seattle
she dreams of the one that got away.

Amusement

We ride them in pursuit of something far
outside our average daily experience
these ten-story death wheels
these perilous whirling vomitoriums
these four-person runaway trains
without an engineer or pilot in sight
assembled in haste by carnies battling
hangovers from last night's trailer blowout.
We ride them to shake up our routine
put a good scare in us, make us scream
make our heart come up into our throat
grip the safety bar like it means something
through loops and turns at breakneck speed
holding on in hopes that we make it through
this horribly fantastic window of amusement.

Jim has three memoirs, *Cretin Boy*, *Dirty Shirt* and *The Portland House*. He also has five poetry collections, *Thoughts from a Line at the DMV, Genetically Speaking, On a Road, Written Life* and *Reciting from Memory*. Jim is a past Poet Laureate for the Village of Wales, WI. Visit:
https://sites.google.com/view/jimlandwehr/home

Sydney Lea

Vermont Poet Laureate, 2011 - 2015

My Wife's Back

All naked but for a strap, it traps my gaze
As we paddle: the dear familiar nubs
Of spine-bone punctuating that sun-warmed swath,

The slender muscles that trouble the same sweet surface.
We've watched and smiled as green herons flushed
And hopped ahead at every bend, and we've looked up

At a redtail tracing open script on a sky
So clear and deep we might believe
It's autumn, no matter it's August still. Another fall

Will be on us before we know it. Of course we adore
That commotion of color, but it seems to come
Again as soon as it's gone away. They all do now.

We're neither young anymore, to put matters plainly.
My love for you over thirty years
Extends in all directions, but now to your back as we drift

And paddle down the tranquil Connecticut River.
We've seen a mink scratch fleas on a mudflat.
We've seen an osprey start to dive but seeing us,

Think better of it. Two phoebes wagged on an ash limb.
Your torso is long. I can't see your legs
But they're longer, I know. Phoebe, osprey, heron, hawk:

Marvels under Black Mountain, but I am fixed
On your back, indifferent to other wonders:
Bright minnows that flared in the shallows,

the gleam off that poor mink's coat,
even the fleas in its fur, the various birds
–the lust of creatures just to survive.

But I watch your back. Never have I wished more not to die.

On the Other Hand (1968)

Aretha's "Natural Woman," andante-funky,
spilled from every window
                              in town that summer.
The weather and people's moods got so bad-ass hot
you dreamed cinematic lagoons and palm trees bowing
to evening's cool sand. You imagined parrot-chatter
in the hills would turn tuneful as you sipped iced drinks with umbrellas.

With your amour. Of course. The lyrical breezes
were soft as the lady's touch.
                              On the other hand,
o, puny Lothario, dime-store virtuoso
of tango, mangler of first-year classroom Spanish,
duty called: there were things that depended on you!
Like tearing the social fabric to pieces, re-weaving

the whole into what in your dotage you understand–
– when you get right down to facts–
                              was your own sorry image.
What's left of hope in this blighted nation is owing
in part to your failures and those of your smug little cohort.
And baby, I don't mean maybe. You knew jack-shit.
You remained romantic imagination's ragdoll.

You'd merely changed your clothes. And now you needed,
                              you thought, what you thought
was ordeal by fire, duress. Solidarity
with the colorful oppressed– that's what defined you.

168

What a laugh and a half looking back. You wanted great change
and you changed nothing. And so, poor narcissist,
your big question's still what it was in those days of ferment:

if your *soul was in the lost and found,* what role
would be the next that *came along to claim it?*

A former Pulitzer finalist, Sydney Lea served was founding editor of *New England Review.* Vermont's Poet Laureate from 2011 to 2015, in 2021, he was presented with his home state of Vermont's most prestigious artist's distinction: the Governor's Award for Excellence in the Arts.

David K. Leff

New England Beat Poet Laureate

Found Ferlinghetti at 100: A Birthday Souvenir

You were a pocket poet in my backpack
at sixteen as I thumbed coast-to-coast
to find *the secret meaning of things*,
daring to cross *all the obscene boundaries*.

Suffering many *unfair arguments*
with existence, for years afterward
I struggled for an *open eye, open heart*.

Decades passed before I knew *how to paint*
sunlight, find *a Buddha in the woodpile*
and keep a *journal for the protection of all beings*.

My Brooklyn-bred dad died in *a Coney*
Island of the mind, teasing me with rhythmic
sea sounds and a scent of fries and salt,
mere *pictures of the gone world*.

I learned that growing older births
landscapes of living and dying that steal
my time and take a bit of world from me.

So I found that *these are my rivers*
—Farmington to Connecticut to sea—

170

and discovered *poetry as an insurgent art*.

It took too long to know that *love*
is no stone on the moon, but the wet, soft,
warmth of my lover's kiss, and the open
road of your poems that led me there.

At the Spam Museum

Pass a boy in bronze walking a pig,
and enter a shrine to American
invention and marketing

in a suburban style shopping plaza
where hallowed historical site
meets glitzy carnival cheer.

Celebrity in a can becomes nutrition
in a feelgood film with upbeat
commercial clips. Antique

containers and old-time ads
are sacred relics beside the founder's
words engraved in glass.

As much metaphor as meat,
it's a worthless email, survivalist shelter
staple, punchline searching for a joke,

weapon of mass consumption
that won the big war for Ike, and Scout
campfire ritual on a stick.

Every bite is what you need it to be,
for a dozen cans a second can't lie.
We are what we eat. Spam I am.

David K. Leff is an award-winning poet and essayist, poet laureate of Canton, Connecticut, and former deputy commissioner of the Connecticut Department of Environmental Protection. He was honored as New England Beat Poet Laureate by the National Beat Poetry Foundation in 2018. By appointment of the National Park Service, David served as poet-in-residence for the New England National Scenic Trail (NET) for 2016-17. The author of six nonfiction books, three volumes of poetry, and two novels in verse, he is poetry editor of *Connecticut Woodlands*, the quarterly of the Connecticut Forest & Park Association. David is a trustee of Great Mountain Forest in Norfolk, Connecticut, a non-profit working forest, and deputy town historian and town meeting moderator of Canton, Connecticut where he also served 26 years as a volunteer firefighter. His papers are located at the Special Collections and University Archives, UMass/Amherst http://scua.library.umass.edu/umarmot/?s=leff View his work at www.davidkleff.com

Elline Lipkin

Poet Laureate of Altadena, California, 2016-2018

O. L.A.

Lost in your maze
of 5s and 10s,
my car is a bead
stringing itself
across your necklace
of highways, curved
and twisting against
your throat, then zippering
up and down the coast.

5, 10, 105, 110,
a thread spins out.
Then 710, 405, 210,
I reel back home.

You have not always
been easy to love:
strip malls and billboards,
a heat that rises off
concrete and clings.

Seasons of no season,
in summer you keep us
locked in. In winter,

exhale us along the beach
to walk the sand's balmy cool.

At dusk, I climb up
into light pink skies,
past the purple trees
shedding spring while
palm trees line the street
crowned against the blue.

You sprawl, parched by sun,
yet pocked with backyard pools,
lounge into sunset and lower
your mirrored sunglasses
to peer above their edge.
Quick flip them up,
again, a mystery.

Elline Lipkin is a poet, academic, and nonfiction writer. Her first book of poems, *The Errant Thread*, was chosen by Eavan Boland for the Kore Press First Book Award. Her second book, *Girls' Studies,* was published by Seal Press. Her poems have been published in various contemporary journals and she has been a resident at Yaddo, the Virginia Center for the Creative Arts, and the Dorland Mountain Arts Colony. From 2016-2018, she served as Poet Laureate of Altadena and co-edited the *Altadena Poetry Review*. Currently a Research Scholar with UCLA's Center for the Study of Women, she has taught poetry workshops for Writing Workshops Los Angeles, Chapman University, Scripps College, and worked online and in the classroom with a variety of writers.

Maria Lisella

<u>Queens, New York Poet Laureate</u>

Our Date

My stepson spent
the afternoon in detention
for lying to a nun.
I told them my name means
pheasants in Italian,
but no one believed me.
Half white, half Puerto Rican,
Italian last name, nappy hair,
said otherwise.
At the perfect age of 10,
my stepson and I
had a date one afternoon.
Determined to teach him to fly,
forget nuns, divorced parents,
over-protective mother,
or, just ride a bike.
A two-wheeler, banana seat,
shiny, chrome, bells, streamers.
He'd run alongside it
throw one leg far and wide
in time to find the peddle
on the other side.
I clutched the back of the seat
sent him off as far as I could.

Like my father did for me,
knowing spills and harm
would follow.
Years later,
a knot in my heart,
his dusty, tear-smeared face
lips quivering, telling me
of a quick ride to an Italian
neighborhood in Pelham Bay
where he was chased down
by taunts of
You don't belong here.
I tried to tell them my name
but no one listened.
I think of all I don't know
about courage – how to build it,
pass it on, when to fight, to flee,
and when to leave your bike
behind, save your life,
find your way home.

Maria Lisella is the sixth Queens Poet Laureate; and is an Academy of American Poets Fellow. She co-curates the Italian American Writers Association series celebrating its 31st year. Her collections include *Thieves in the Family, Amore on Hope Street* and *Two Naked Feet; The Man with a* Plan is forthcoming. She featured on "The Poet and The Poem" from the Library of Congress.

Radomir Vojtech Luza

__Poet Laureate of North Hollywood, California__

Halloween Saturday Night, 2020, At 6:07 p.m.

Instead of gargoyles and ghouls
Witches and warlocks invade schools.

Sky reddish pink and royal blue
Mixing with North Hollywood's
bright green hue.

A sacred stew of me and you.

A heavy crew looking for life anew.

Among this COVID clue
ending at the local zoo.

Moon full as a burning head
Glowing like flaming lead.

Alabaster clouds puffy
Lush trees fluffy.

Standing like royal sentries at state ball.

Pushing hour back for some slack.

Frightened that life will not grow.
Fit to tow my grit
Or ease this quit in my pit.

Darkness do not drive me tonight.
Instead turn to water and light
windmill and kite.

At earliest sight as dawn turns
the rabbit right.

Radomir Vojtech Luza was born in Vienna, Austria in 1963 to renowned Czech parents. The SAG/AFTRA/AEA union actor, veteran stand-up comedian, theatre, film, book critic and host has been the Poet Laureate of North Hollywood, CA since 2012, and the author of thirty-one books, (twenty-seven collections of poetry), the latest of which MENTAL MALL, a twenty poem chapbook published by Four Feathers Press in Pasadena, CA this past August. The sports and freelance writer is a graduate of Jesuit High School and Tulane University (New Orleans, LA). The organizer, host and curator of fifteen poetry readings in places such as Jersey City, New Jersey; Hoboken, New Jersey; New York City; Fort Walton Beach, FL; and Los Angeles has his thirty-second book, (28th Collection of Poetry) ONYX ROSE forthcoming later this year or early next year from Westbow Press. Luza is also the editor and publisher of the literary journal VOICES IN THE LIBRARY, published by Red Doubloon Publishing, the literary arm of Radman Productions. Luza, who has recorded nine spoken word CD's has also published over seventy poems in literary journals, anthologies, websites and other media. He has featured his poetry over one hundred times across the country.

Mary McElveen

Poet Laureate for Alexandria, Virginia 2007-2010

Junk Drawer

Two wrenches, one ruler.
One stapler, jammed.
Fifteen pens and a lonely highlighter.
Pruning shears, small,
recently released from incarceration
in the garden shed.
Gift cards, business cards,
appointment cards. A hammer.
A Leatherman: the awkward
Jack-of-all-tools, but master of none.
Packages of tiny beads that morph
into marble-sized colored spheres
amazing all and sundry, but mostly me.
Allen wrenches and Lilliputian
screwdrivers for delicate jobs...
A box cutter for less-demanding ones.
One Noah figure
(and one Noah arm)
inexplicably separated on the ark.
Scotch tape, duct tape, decorative tape,
sticking together through thick and thin.
Keys. More keys. and yet more keys
unlocking the secrets of the ages..
or the back door of another house.

Receipts. Coupons. Phone numbers.
Twelve small black pellets of mysterious origin
and no apparent use.
A veritable variety store
of pennies, buttons, magnets,
pins, binder clips, matches,
sticky notes.

And two harmonicas
Humming sad histories of
the forgotten.

King Tut—2020

We've been buried for a month or more,
and it's gotten old.
This tomb has lots of distractions
(I'm reminded of the pyramids):
but nothing like the world we knew.
No matter how many gadgets and gew-gaws,
the fact remains: we're stuck.

There's food, there are books, there is
the inevitable television,
(which the pharaohs were spared)
replete with news and politics
and assorted drivel
that would bore us to death, if we weren't
already dead and buried.

So here we sit, lined up nicely
in our nice, neat boxes--
veritable mummies, wrapped in
anti-virus masks, antiseptic wipes, and fear,
drumming our freshly-washed fingers,
impatiently awaiting
       resurrection.

Mary McElveen is a former Poet Laureate for the City of Alexandria (2007-2010). As such, she has written poetry for dedications of cemeteries, high school renovations, recreation centers, awards ceremonies—and just about anything you'd care to name. She has also enjoyed a number of disparate careers: mom, school volunteer, PTA president, biochemist, chemistry researcher, high school chemistry teacher and science department chair, tech support for a major financial institution, tech education resource, and has acted as director for office support and lawyer referral at a local bar association. She volunteers and gives tours as a docent at the Folger Shakespeare Library in Washington, D.C. She is also a member of the Grolier Club, America's oldest and largest society for bibliophiles and enthusiasts in the graphic arts. In her spare time, she writes.

John F. McMullen

Poet Laureate of the Town of Yorktown, New York

A Poem Is Not A Jump Shot

I have done at least
one thing perfectly
in my life
I have faked my man
gone up in the air and
gotten nothing by net
perfect
Now I write poetry
and now no matter
how happy I am
with a poem
it is never perfect
It can always be tweaked
have words added
or cut or changed
never really finished
never perfect
But, sometimes,
I have
    to pause
    to stop
and just get
poems out the door
And that is this submission

John F. McMullen, *"johnmac the bard"*, is the Poet Laureate of the Town of Yorktown, NY, an adjunct professor at Westchester Community College, a graduate of Iona College, the holder of two Masters degrees from Marist College, a member of the American Academy of Poets and Poets & Writers, the author of over 2,500 columns and articles and 10 books (*8 poetry*), a contributor to a many magazines, journals & anthologies (*including three from Local Gems Press*) and the host of a weekly Internet Radio Show (*300 episodes to date*).

Daniel McTaggart

West Virginia Beat Poet Laureate, 2017 - 2019

A Gathering Of Uncles

The farmhouse kitchen became a mystery
When old men smoked fat cigars after dinner
Beneath a plaster ceiling
Stained with a whiskey sour glow.

Conversation curled with every breath.
I left when the air stung my eyes
To read comics with coffee rings on them.

I heard grandpa and his brothers-in-law
Laughing like diesel carburetors
Coughing up carbon in a small humid room
As another puff of smoke pushed

Through all the previous whispers.
I couldn't tell how they were smiling.
Only that they were.

The Neighbor Kid

He helped me cut branches off
Old pine trees his dad planted above a wall

His three grandkids couldn't imagine
Undergrowth almost ten times older than them

I remember stopping by his house every Halloween
His dad gave out bags of potato chips from work

Man, that was the best

He recalled playing whiffleball with his brother
Just below where we stood

He reached down in a thatch of ground vines
Picked up a plastic sphere laying there for decades

Either he or his brother hit it
And he just caught a 50-year line drive

Daniel McTaggart served as the West Virginia Beat Poet Laureate from 2017 to 2019. His poetry has appeared in Amomancies, Backbone Mountain Review, and Kestrel. His book "Midnight Muse in a Convenience Store" is available from Venetian Spider Press. He can usually be found writing in bookstores, diners, and local coffee shops."

Caryn Mirriam-Goldberg

Kansas Poet Laureate, 2009-2013

The Thread

My mother singing "Tora Lora Lora,"
an Irish lullaby although we were Brooklyn Jews.
The vacuum's roar muffled by shag carpeting
while the birch banged on the hapless window sill.
The humming refrigerator in the middle of the night
when everyone slept or paced alone in the old house.
The chants encasing me in each swaying note
as I wrapped my thin arms around my cold chest
in the cavernous synagogue. The creak of the swing
as I turned horizontal, defying gravity in the static
of the transistor radio. The old staccato of my father's anger.
The loud slap on the bass notes of the bare torso
making new bruises, then the slow breath pacing in
until the danger was gone. All the possibilities in each
novel about a girl born afraid but about to enter the calm pond
of my life and swim. Bike tires on wet pavement at dawn.
The first kiss in the back of the school bus broken by applause.
How rain parts its pouring for thunder's interior roar.
The mornings revved up like motorcycles, the exhaling speed
of rivers, starving for new ground or betrayed by rocks
toward the remembering willows, singing reed by reed.
The happy rhythm of the subway rocking my spine
in and out of alignment with the dark, tunneling through water,
all the buzzing bodies ferrying millions of cells into sound,
the miracle of one rushing animal carrying us all.

How To See

You think the way you see is a commons,
right in the middle of a Midwestern college town
where all the regular Joes mill about, calling out
"Daffodil!", "Blue bench!", "Red coffee mug still warm!"

You think we all see the same stream to the left
winding through moss where someone planted
one jonquil in 1967, now turned into a thousand,
and to the right, a freshly-built housing complex
with matching faux balconies and red trim.

On the cobblestone plaza someone laid 100 years ago,
you think you see nothing but the yellow wrapper
of a cough drop, and later, someone's three-year-old,
squatted low, reaching out to catch what he can't
of cottonwood fluff before it turns to snow.

You don't remember learning to see in the womb,
a pale shadow of someone approaching
or the tight space between where your mother ends
and the car dashboard begins until the violent
disruption of light that doesn't soften, only sharpens
until you are old, looking away from the crowd
at the leggy creek where water winds over rock.

None or all of what you see is you: the tendrils
of earth and all its DNA in its variety pack of spirals
winding through time, or is it time exhaling
into another blossoming lily-of-the-valley,
or months before, melting black snow
on the street where you first lived?

Maybe sight has always been a great lake,
too cold, even in summer, in swim, but look!
You can lean on this rock, a remnant of magma,
stop measuring your life in beauty, and love
the distance turning gold, then orange, then blue.

Caryn Mirriam-Goldberg, Ph.D., the 2009-13 Kansas Poet Laureate is the author of 24 books, including *How Time Moves: New & Selected Poems*; *Miriam's Well*, a novel; *Needle in the Bone,* a non-fiction book on the Holocaust; *The Sky Begins At Your Feet: A Memoir on Cancer, Community, and Coming Home to the Body*. Founder of Transformative Language Arts, she leads writing workshops widely, coaches people on writing and right livelihood, and consults on creativity. YourRightLivelihood.com, Bravevoice.com, CarynMirriamGoldberg.com

karla k. morton

Texas Poet Laureate, 2010

Aperçu

You ask me to sum up this manuscript
in 90 seconds –
a ride in an elevator,
200 words or less.

But this is a book of *poems* –
those things lodged in the heart
brought on by bacon and chocolate
and war and kids that miss their curfew
and sisters dying
and a kiss that punctures façade.

And they're for *you* – to roll in,
to swallow, to seep in your bloodstream
and pound open the chamber doors
of your own heart.

They are interior dwellers –
those things that rise in your chest;
that suffer the back of your throat till you
speak their name.

They are memory and breath and need.
They are the 88 spring times we wish

we could have;
the lush grape before the wine,
the stained lips after.

*apercu – a glimpse, insight, or summary

First published in *Accidental Origami: New and Selected Works by karla k. morton* (Texas Review Press)

---

karla k. morton has fifteen books, and is nominated for the National Cowgirl Hall of Fame. Her *"The National Parks: A Century of Grace"* (TCU Press) with fellow Poet Laureate Alan Birkelbach, is historic: there's never been another poetry book written in-situ from each of the 62 National Parks to help culturally preserve and protect these sacred spaces for the next seven generations. Her most recent poetry book *"Politics of the Minotaur"* has just won the Spur Award from the WWA and the Firebird Book Award. A National Heritage Wrangler Award Winner, Foreword Book of the Year Award winner, and twice a Next Generation Indie National Book Award winner, she's published in journals such as *American Life in Poetry, Alaska Quarterly Review, Arkansas Review, Southword, descant, Boulevard, Comstock Review, Lascaux Review,New Ohio Review* and *Right Hand Pointing*. She was named Texas Poet Laureate in 2010.

Tom Murphy

<u>Corpus Christi, Texas, Poet Laureate 2021-2022</u>

About the Mask

Only have one bought mask. The rest were given
and many home-made. Most of the given are too thin
as well as the bought, "You shall not pass!" Gandalf
mask with floating Covid-19 viruses battered back
by his staff on the Bridge of Khazad-Dûm.

Sarah, Gail and Janet hand sowed masks and gave
them away. The one that I use most come from Janet B.
Some rip my hair out, some burn the back of my ears.
Having to teach through them for classes face to face
while other students are synchronistical online —

fogging up glasses, feeling suffocated at times.
That one instant I appear without a mask, upon arrival
handed a paper medical turquoise one that hid my shame
from the tsk-tsk. For nine months so far with no end in sight.
I may not like wearing a mask, but I sure do love living.

Tom Murphy is the 2021-2022 Corpus Christi Poet Laureate and the *Langdon Review*'s 2022 Writer-In-Residence. Murphy's books: *When I Wear Bob Kaufman's Eyes* (2022) from Gnashing Teeth Publishing, *Snake Woman Moon* (2021), *Pearl* (2020), *American History* (2017), and co-edited *Stone Renga* (2017) with Alan Berecka. He's been published widely in literary journals and anthologies such as: *Poetry is DEAD: An Inclusive Anthology of Deadhead Poetry, Boundless, Concho River Review, MONO, Good Cop/Bad Cop Anthology, Odes and Elegies: Eco-Poetry from the Texas Gulf Coast, Wine Anthology, The Great American Wise Ass Poetry Anthology, Red River Review, Switchgrass Review, Windward Review, Corpus Christi Writers Anthologies, Voice de la Luna, WordFest Anthology, Outrage: A Protest Anthology for Injustice in a Post 9/11 World* among other publications. Recently retired from Texas A&M University-Corpus Christi, he still works with the Barrio Writers and the People's Poetry Festival. Contact information, books or bookings tom@tommurphywriter.com https://tommurphywriter.com

Abby E. Murray

Tacoma, Washington, Poet Laureate 2019-2021

Short Lectures on Hope

Some of us
inherit hope.
Some of us
dip our doubt
in gold paint.

*

I like hope.
It sounds
more livable
than *waiting*
or *wanting*.

*

Is hope
cliché?
I suppose.
So is
breathing.

*

It turns out
my problem
is with people
who dismiss
clichés.

*

It's easy
to dislike
what's constant:
clichés, mothers,
death, souls.

*

When I was little
I thought the soul
was a sword
only death could
pull from you.

*

I thought hope
was a yellow fruit
that grew in
a husk you weren't
supposed to eat.

*

This is what
happens when
you tell a kid
to go play
and be quiet.

*

She turns
your words
back into
what they
were before.

*

I have ruined
this poem
more times
than I have
written it.

*

To survive is
to carry
a story.
To hope is
to set it down.

Abby E. Murray is the editor of *Collateral*, a literary journal concerned with the impact of violent conflict and military service beyond the combat zone. Her book, *Hail and Farewell*, won the Perugia Press Poetry Prize and was a finalist for the 2020 Washington State Book Award. She teaches (remotely) rhetoric in military strategy to Army War College fellows at the University of Washington. After serving as poet laureate for the city of Tacoma, Washington, she recently relocated to Washington DC, where her spouse works in the Pentagon.

Tammy Nuzzo-Morgan

Suffolk County, New York Poet Laureate 2009-2011

I Couldn't Write a Poem Because

The birds are flocking in oranging trees
It is Friday
I am fifty-seven years old
My phone keeps ringing
The midterms are over
It isn't my birthday
My daughter just got a great job
My neighbor is building an addition
Regular gas is $2.85 a gallon
I live on Long Island
My son lives in Harlem
My cat is mean
I ran out of coffee creamer
Rich Hoffman says it won't rain today
My husband just kissed me
I'm working on my dissertation
My friend came over for lunch
I teach Freshman English Comp
I cannot win spider solitaire
You aren't here

How to Write a Poem

Begin with the lump in your throat,
the anguish in your heart,
let it simmer, swell, seep into your bones.

Set it aside and look for the proper container:
form, lyrical, free verse. Make sure you wash the
remnants of other poems cleanly away.

Use adjective, adverbs, prepositions and
articles sparingly; these are useless and signal
you do not trust your guest's discerning taste.

Open your salty rivers, let just enough to
flow into your mixture, allow verbs and
nouns to bring forth clear images.

Stir imagination into the mix deftly until thickened
into a poem which can stand on its own,
and the guest can savor the pain.

Put your creation out to cool on the windowsill.
Be sure to watch out for pecking birds who would
delight in devouring your creation.

After the heat has dissipated give your prize a second look
for any imperfections, dust off, place into a tidy title box,
finally, wrap your name around in the shape of a bow.

Tammy Nuzzo-Morgan is the first woman to be appointed Suffolk County Poet Laureate (2009-2011). She awarded by the Walt Whitman Birthplace the title of 2017 Long Island Poet of the Year. She is the founder and president of Long Island Poetry & Literature Repository. Tammy, who already holds a Master of Business Administration degree, has also completed a Master of Fine Arts degree from Stony Brook University Southampton. She has earned her Ph.D. in Humanities & Culture in the Interdisciplinary Studies program at Union Institute & University. Her dissertation was on: The Healing Power of Poetry. She teaches at Long Island University at the C W Post campus. She maintains an active schedule of workshops and performances.

Linda Opyr

**Nassau County, New York, Poet Laureate, 2011-2013**

Something Changed

The light shifted
into shards of shadow.

The trees spread their dark sides
to the earth before me.

How will I breathe
when your breath is gone?

Late Afternoon, The Wind Cold

Small girl crying at the door,
what do you keep inside?

Red leaf floating in the wind,
why am I so heavy?

One stone upon the other,
why questions I cannot answer?

Linda Opyr was the Nassau County Poet Laureate 2011-13. She is the author of eight collections of poetry, most recently Where the Eye Wants Coast (2020). Her poems have appeared in *Poetry Ireland Review*, *The Hudson Review*, *The Atlanta Review*, *the Paterson Literary Review,* and *The New York Times*, as well as other publications in Ireland, Wales, England and the United States. In 2017 she was a featured poet at the Bailieborough Poetry Festival in County Cavan, Ireland.

Carlo Parcelli

Maryland Beat Poet Laureate Emeritus

Empedocles on the Dulles Parkway

The Pentagon was built in 1941,
  In the beginning
 Of the last slug fest America thinks it won.
Grudgingly abetting the Soviets
   In their Great Patriotic War
  Became the bogey at the center
    Of the American panopticon
Which concluded millions of lives, subito,
  Those who have been here and gone.
 And among these bones
   Our poet's heuristic overtones.
Rag picker to the stars;
   Street sweep of the holy satyrs,
Among the women's imperious chatter
  About maids and nannies
   Prep schools and working class slatterns;
Where he on Porter Street met
  James Jesus Angleton sucking on a cigarette
And an addled Allen Dulles,
  Like a ghost wreathed in smoke.
Stuttering a quizzical hello and
   Presenting a limp, doubtful hand
  In this sad, little vignette.
"You know," Angleton said, "John and I

204

Had a go at your man Pound
At Yale in a magazine called Furioso.
   But I'm certain Rudd has you familiar with all of that.
Of matters Pound I hear you're quite the talib.
   Stick with it and someday you too may be as renowned.
Reliving another man's life in prose and verse.
      I can think of worse ways
To spend our measure upon this earth."
   And the sense of loathing and nausea
      That rose in our dear boy.
A brooding evil and the capriciousness of fate
      That would elevate two so insidious
         And, frankly, sorry American reprobates.
And gazing upon these dismal demigods
      Dressed in ash like desolated bums
   Waiting for their kingdom to come,
He thought of Beckett and his 'boy'
         Standing before Didi and Gogo,
   And gave a sick, bewildered look at his host
Who drew on his fag and
   Through eyes, lids half drawn from smoke,
Faintly grinned as if to say 'Here now.
                  I've sucked you in'.
But as Godot does not beat the boy
      But only his brother and the brother
That tends his sheep off stage is bred of
   What the matron's above mean
         By 'maid' and 'nanny',
The kind their husbands prefer to fuck or kill;
         If you will - the 'other'.
   And before Pozzo delivers Lucky a blow,
And fate to masque irony, Lucky shin kicks Gogo,
   Who's already been throttled by hooligans,

And all the ugliness and violence, the futility,
    The rag and bones these three spooks portend;
The poet conjures Samuel's play and says
     "Mr. Godot told me to tell you
        He won't be coming today,
           But surely to-morrow."
     And the shepherd boy turned to go.
There was no pithy quote from Shakespeare or Marlowe,
     Or risible blindside from Bierce or Cocteau.
No, no one stopped him,
       No one raised a hand to slow
          His exit.

Carlo Parcelli is a poet living in the Washington DC area. He is Beat Poet Laureate Emeritus for Maryland & an editor with the literary journal www.flashpointmag.com. He has published 6 books of poetry & has appeared in numerous literary journals.

Linda Pastan

Maryland Poet Laureate, Emeritus

My Obituary

Will it merit a full column in The _Post or_ The _Times_
or just a squib by a relative late for work?
Will it mention awards I didn't win,
poems that didn't quite scan,
and how a student asked me once
if "To a Daughter Leaving Home"
was my penance for driving a daughter away?
It will surely say I was born in the Bronx,
spending the first few weeks of my life
in the hospital nursery, alone. Which may
account for my chronic melancholy
and why I keep blaming my surgeon father
who tried to do his best for me
but whose anger always mirrored mine.
Some obituaries written years in advance
are stored in the newspaper's basement vault,
like turkey vultures asleep in their nests,
just waiting for death to catch up with life.
Let any newspaper where my obituary appears
be used to keep the floor clean under the dog's dish.
And let my "survived by…" children remember me
not by a list of ambiguous facts collected
like so much mathematical data, but by my usual
obsessions: rising bread and falling leaves.

Linda Pastan grew up in New York City, graduated from Radcliffe College in 1954, and received an MA from Brandeis University. She has published 15 volumes of poetry, most recently *Insomnia* which won the Towson University Literary Award and *A Dog Runs Through It.* Two of her books have been finalists for the National Book Award, one for The Los Angeles Times Book Prize. She taught for several years at American University and was on the staff of the Bread Loaf Writer's Conference for 20 years. She is a past Poet Laureate of Maryland. Pastan has won numerous awards, including The Radcliffe Distinguished Alumni Award and The Maurice English Award. In 2003 she won the Ruth Lilly Poetry Prize for lifetime achievement. Pastan lives with her husband in Maryland. They have 3 children and 7 grandchildren.

Alexandria Peary

New Hampshire Poet Laureate

"The Fish," on a Plate

The fish, all forty lines
like feathery bones fanned out
on a plate of unpolished silver, a shield or hubcap
displayed by Coptic Peter tableside.
[C]row-blue mussel shells
bespattered jelly fish, crabs like green / lilies
is served with timber by Marsden Hartley,
a crisscross of fallen men, medals
and ribbons along with Marsden Hartley's Heart,
decorated, —parsley of elms.

All forty lines of the Fish
an ichthys formed by Greek letters,
a secret sign, sprinkled with salt
from Sand Hill back home in Augusta,
ME, poured from a cathedral amid triple-deckers,
a Neruda tomato and Greek poet coffee,
overturned cup, a mess of lemons.
[C]hasm-side, the one who will always get away,
American shad, eel, Alewife
Blueback herring, Rainbow smelt
Tomcod, sea lamprey, the sign of the fish
near licenses plates—3 o'clock traffic.

Alexandria Peary (MFA, MFA, PhD) serves as New Hampshire Poet Laureate. She is the author of nine books, including *The Water Draft, Control Bird Alt Delete, Prolific Moment: Theory and Practice of Mindfulness for Writing,* and *Battle of Silicon Valley at Daybreak.* She is the recipient of a 2020 Academy of American Poets Laureate Fellowship and a specialist in mindful writing.

Tony Pena

Beacon, New York ,Poet Laureate 2017-2018

Farewell Party

Some days I simply
missed you but most
days I longed
like the night
panting for the stars
on an overcast evening.

Damaged as we were,
solace the soothing
ointment of choice
but it takes two
to tango no matter
the steps of the dance.

Somewhere along
the line a familiar
stranger cut in,
changing the sweet
dark where whispers
lit up our souls to these

see your breath
mornings where
the best of intentions

die as myths leaving
the damned to do
what they do best.

Noir Boy

I'm no tough guy
in the Sam Spade
sense of the words,
preferring to leave
the hard boiled
to the eggs
in a Lee J. Cobb
salad but I do love
basking in the black,
grey, and white
shades of a sinful
city donning a dark
halo like Bogey wears
a Borsalino fedora.
Down and close over
the eyes so nobody gets
a clear shot at shattering
the window to my soul
with a silver bullet
from a snub nose 44.

Tony Pena was formerly 2017-2018 Poet Laureate for the city of Beacon, New York. His work has appeared in several publications over the years including Best of the Net nominations in 2019. A volume of poetry and flash fiction, "Blood and Beats and Rock n Roll," is available at Amazon. A chapbook of poetry, "Opening night in Gehenna," is available from author.

Juan Manuel Pérez

**Corpus Christi, Texas, Poet Laureate 2019-2020**

Ode To Rosa Parks

She wasn't the first to take a stand
For our just and natural right
But she made it stick by sitting down
That is how she joined the fight

One eventful, cold December day
She decided she had enough
The world will have to listen now
Even though this might be tough

The white man said you've got to move
To the back is where you'll go
You know the rules, it is the law
Stand quickly now and don't be slow

That fateful day she did not move
And disobeyed the distraught man
The policemen came and arrested her
Forcing her to play by an unjust plan

It didn't matter for time would tell
That she was right to take her stand
Our civil rights became stronger still
From Montgomery to Selma to Birmingham

Swing

reflection from an excerpt of the book
The Boys In The Boat by Daniel James Brown
…as well as, current events

"Poetry, that's what a good 'swing' feels like"
Like rowing, eight in blissful unison
Without missing a single beat at all
A heart beating as one, beating as one
Rowing into blissful oblivion
One that just might have a probable end
Or does it? Maybe Heaven, perhaps hell
Peace or war, life or death, joy or sorrow
Rowing against fear and polarity
Whatever is the most current affair
Rhetoric so fluid like blood on fire
Hand gestures signaling our common state
Whether then or now, we all strive for swing
Which way will you row? How fast will you go?

Juan Manuel Pérez, a Mexican-American poet of indigenous descent and the current Poet Laureate for Corpus Christi, Texas (2019-2020), is the author of several books of poetry including two new books, SPACE IN PIECES (The House Of The Fighting Chupacabras Press, 2020) and SCREW THE WALL! AND OTHER BROWN PEOPLE POEMS (FlowerSong Press, 2020).

Octavio Quintanilla

San Antonio, Texas, Poet Laureate 2018-2020

Poem Writing A Suicide Note

By the time you begin
writing this poem,

your father is dead.

This time, it's for real.
Unlike that poem you wrote

in which you have him fall
from a ladder, cracks

his head, loses memory,
but doesn't die.

In another poem, he is
a construction worker,

South Texas sunlight
hammering his back,

dies in the end.
For you, it was all pretend.

Most of your adult life
you've been like a five-year old

child, pretending patricide,
documenting it in poems,

all the while afraid to dirty
your hands with true blood.

Keep pretending to be five
and offer your testicles

to his inspection.
How silly you feel in this memory,

such a tough guy now,
knowing there was nothing

shameful or perverse about it,
just a man making sure his son

had the balls to rise against him,
if necessary.

How much more pretending
must you do?

How small you are
in that mortgage

you'll never finish paying.
The student loans you drag

to bed every night.
How much longer will you pretend

the world does everything right
and all you do in the world

is wrong? If you could only believe,
one last time, that missing someone

can be infinite, can outlive you.
Pretend, for your sake,

that maybe it does.
that maybe it doesn't.

Octavio Quintanilla is the author of the poetry collection, *If I Go Missing* (Slough Press, 2014) and served as the 2018-2020 Poet Laureate of San Antonio, TX. His poetry, fiction, translations, and photography have appeared in numerous journals and his visual work has been exhibited at the Southwest School of Art, Presa House Gallery, the Brownsville Museum of Fine Art, and many other art spaces. Octavio teaches Literature and Creative Writing in the M.A./M.F.A. program at Our Lady of the Lake University in San Antonio, Texas. Website: https://www.octavioquintanilla.com/

Kevin Rabis

__Poet Laureate of Kansas 2017-2019__

musical

Gray day, after
  the long rain, everything
green, and inside, dry,
he sings the first
  few words of "Love
a Rainy Night,"
  by Eddie Rabbitt,
and she says, "Enough.
It's not raining.
And it's not night."

our town

And the days lay down
  like wheat
in the rain, hard rain,
  and you get in your car
and drive: and what
  do you do
with the night?

Poet Laureate of Kansas (2017-2019) Kevin Rabas teaches at Emporia State University, where he leads the poetry and playwriting tracks and chairs the Department of English, Modern Languages, and Journalism. He has twelve books, including *Lisa's Flying Electric Piano*, a Kansas Notable Book and Nelson Poetry Book Award winner; *All That Jazz;* and *Everyone Just Wants to Drum*. He is the recipient of the Emporia State President's Award for Research and Creativity and is the winner of the Langston Hughes Award for Poetry and the Salina New Voice Award.

Sam Ragan

North Carolina Poet Laureate, Emeritus

The Election

He didn't get drunk
But once every four years,
On election day.
He would rise early and go
To the polls drinking hard
All day. By the time
The polls were closed
He would be passed out.
It was his way of expressing an opinion.

Sandhills Summer

They say the sea was once here.
And sometimes at night
When the wind is rising
I can hear the sea's surge
In the sound of the pines.

You have gathered the brown branches
Which bear the pink blossoms
And I watch you arrange them
In a green bowl.
Your hands ask questions
And then give the answers.

It is very still tonight,
Before morning there will be rain.
The only sound is the cry of the cat
Wanting to come in.

I sleep under the shadow of ghost winds.

Sam Ragan (1915-1996) was a well-known journalist, poet and arts advocate in North Carolina, the state's first Secretary of Cultural Resources , Chairman of the NC Arts Council, NC's Poet Laureate, and recipient of the Roanoke-Chowan Award for his book of collected poems. His literary column Southern Accent ran for 48 years and he is fondly known as " North Carolina's Literary Godfather. "

Thelma T. Reyna

Altadena, California Poet Laureate 2014-2016

Trembling Leaf

A trembling leaf on my orange tree
tells me there's a village scout
in the branch, a faithful worker
in a velour suit seeking sweetness
for his queen and comrades
back at the hive.

So I await with breath abated, bending,
peering at the aromatic tremor,
waiting for the blur and buzz of
the seeker to appear.

He emerges smiling, triumphant,
but not before shaking things some more.
Suit pristine, shoes dusty with his work,
he shows off dance moves
on the airy floor, then butts his hips
on a few more leaves and weaves away.

No, he's not drunk with nectar,
just an emissary as we all are,
from queen or gods, joyful in due
diligence, in doing for others.

Originally published in the author's book, *Dearest Papa: A Memoir in Poems.* (Golden Foothills Press, 2020).

Thelma T. Reyna's books have collectively won 16 national literary awards. She has written six books: a short story collection, *The Heavens Weep for Us and Other Stories;* two poetry chapbooks—*Breath & Bone* and *Hearts in Common;* and three full-length poetry collections—*Rising, Falling, All of Us; Reading Tea Leaves After Trump*; and *Dearest Papa: A Memoir in Poems.* She has edited three anthologies, comprising about 200 poets: As Poet Laureate in Altadena, 2014-2016, she edited the *Altadena Poetry Review Anthology* in 2015 and 2016; and her curated anthology, *When the Virus Came Calling: COVID-19 Strikes America,* was released in September 2020. Thelma's fiction, poetry, and nonfiction have appeared in literary journals, anthologies, textbooks, blogs, and regional media, print and online, for over 25 years. She was a Pushcart Prize Nominee in Poetry in 2017. She received her Ph.D. from UCLA.

Paul Richmond

National Beat Poet Laureate, United States 2019 – 2020
Beat Poet Laureate, Massachusetts 2017 - 2019

Normal

As a little girl
She found herself
Banging on everything
She encountered

She wanted to hear what it sounded like
She was always searching for sounds
It drove her mother crazy
She was always asking her to stop
Asking her
Can't you be normal

She didn't listen to her mother
She listened to the sounds
She became the most vanguard musical performer
Who would go into a rage
On hearing the word normal

Her music
We had never heard anything like it
She was letting us hear
What she heard
And everyone who was around her
Learned never to use the word normal

Germs Are Everywhere

He was squatting
At a river bank
Dipping his toothbrush
Into the river
To brush his teeth

Above stream
A man
For some reason was shitting
In the river

He was interrupted
As a bloated cow
Floated down the river

Some people
Worry about germs

Paul was named Beat Poet Laureate twice, Massachusetts 2017 to 2019, and then U S National Beat Poet Laureate 2019 - 2020. He is best described as political, deadpan and wryly humorous delivered in his own style. He has been called, "Assassin of Apathy – power of words / humor - on the unthinkable, the unsolvable, to analyze to digest to give birth to creativity and hope." He has performed nationally and internationally as a featured poet: The Austin International Poetry Festival, at the Jazzköltexzeti est in Budapest, Hungary. at the Beat Festival Stockholm, Sweden, at the Edinburgh Fringe Festival Scotland, at the Massachusetts Poetry Festival, at West End Poetry Festival NC, in Senegal, Africa with the Senegal – American project, and at the National Beat Poetry Festival. Paul was also in the movie "Trash" by Bucky Jones as a poet. Www.humanerrorpublishing.com

Luis J. Rodriguez

Los Angeles, California Poet Laureate 2014-2016

Make a Poem Cry

"I can't see 'em coming from my eye, so I had to make this poem cry."
—Jimmy McMillan, an incarcerated poet in California's prison system.

You can chain the body, the face, the eyes,
the way hands move coarsely over cement
or deftly on tattooed skin with needle.
You can cage the withered membrane,
the withered dream,
the way razor wire, shouts, yells, and batons
can wither spirit.

But how can you imprison a poem?
How can a melody be locked up, locked down?
Yes, even caged birds sing,
even grass sprouts through asphalt,
even a flower blooms in a desert.

And the gardens of trauma we call the incarcerated
can also spring with the vitality of a deep thought,
an emotion buried beneath the facades
deep as rage, deep as grief,
the grief beneath all rages.

The blood of such poems, songs,

228

emotions, thoughts, dances,
are what flow in all art, stages, films, books.

The keys to liberation are in the heart,
in the mind, behind the cranial sky.
The imagination is boundless,
the inexhaustible in any imprisoned system.

And remember—we are all in some kind of prison.

If only the contrived freedoms
society professes can flow from such water!

Luis J. Rodriguez served as Los Angeles Poet Laureate from 2014-2016. He has 16 books in poetry, fiction, nonfiction, and children's literature. He's founding editor of Tia Chucha Press and co-founder of Tia Chucha's Centro Cultural & Bookstore in L.A.'s San Fernando Valley. His awards include a Carl Sandburg Book Award, a Lila Wallace-Reader's Digest Writing Award, a Passaic Poetry Book Award, and fellowships from the Lannan Foundation, North Carolina, Illinois, California, Chicago, and Los Angeles, among others. His last poetry book is "Borrowed Bones (2015 Curbstone Books/Northwestern University Press). His latest book is "From Our Land to Our Land: Essays, Journeys & Imaginings of a Native Xicanx Writer" (2020 Seven Stories Press).

Margaret Rozga

Wisconsin Poet Laureate 2019-2020

Morning Prayer

Dear God of green unfolding
up out of the earth, what strength in tiny gentle
Dear God of small children
Dear God of laughter, lists, longing, and litanies
Dear God of those who will die before
they have a chance to claim a place on this earth
Dear God, anthropomorphized
almost beyond recognition
Dear God of children crying for their parents
Dear God of my unbelief
Dear God of stories
Dear God of the faint rose-gold light rising
at the lake's eastern shore
Dear God who hums, almost inaudibly
who hums along the bend in the river
who sets humming going, who sets song going
who doesn't sing along
Dear God of crying parents
Dear God who, dear God of, dear God, what,
when, where. Dear God, why
Dear God, I   dear God, not I   dear God, you
Dear God, we, us
Dear God, them
Dear God, why

Dear God of the worm and the whale
Dear God by the book and the unwritten
the spoken and the not yet imagined
the crop come to fruition, eaten,
digested, and become one
with she who prays by paying attention
when words ring false, too small or too big,
twisted or ironed flat
Dear God, what strength

Margaret Rozga, 2019-2020 Wisconsin Poet Laureate, creates poetry from her ongoing concern for social justice issues. Her fifth collection of poetry, *Holding My Selves Together: New and Selected Poems,* will launch in spring 2021 from Cornerstone Press.

Raúl Sánchez

__Redmond, Washington Poet Laureate__

Resurrection

At half-staff, the flag waved in the air
that century old air, that eternal air, dangerous air.
Survival is a matter of priority
But dying while breathing?
An impossible story of resurrection
to test my beliefs, to prove
that the world has not lost its embrace
for all of us despite the pain—

The annuals return every spring
not always wearing their glorious colors
nor the petunias blossoming at the root
of magnolia and maple trees.
Their resurrection is not impossible—
muted on the ground along
the roots of dogwood and maple
resurrection seems possible.

But who am I to speak about that
which I've never experienced—
will I come back next year as a blossoming crocus?
Or a dandelion weed?

I want to touch the serrated leaves
of the nettle stalks and the poison oak
to prove I'm alive! And feel
the pain of living.

Raúl is the current City of Redmond Poet Laureate. He teaches poetry in Spanish at Evergreen High School through the Seattle Arts and Lectures (WITS) program, also at Denny International Middle School through the Jack Straw Educational Project and volunteers for PONGO Teen Writing at the Juvenile Detention Center.

Hayden Saunier

Bucks County, Pennsylvania Poet Laureate Emeritus

Say Luck

Since you are alive and have leisure enough to read poems
I'd say luck has entered your life more than once

unless this is the first poem you've read. If it is, well,
I'm sorry, but still, you're alive and that involves

Luck and her trusty companion, Split Second Timing.
Remember those movies in health class; remember

the odds for each egg, each spermatazoan? This morning
I woke determined to write a poem about love:

in my dream I'd crossed over a bridge like the bridge
by a slow moving river where my boyfriend

from high school and I used to park. I wanted to
slide slowly down the slick Naugahyde seats of that car—

writing does that—takes you back, makes you look
odd things up, like how to spell Naugahyde—

and the first poem everyone reads should be about
love. Not luck. And not trees. I mean no offense

234

to Joyce Kilmer, who was—did you know this?—
a man. Alfred Joyce Kilmer, writer, editor, poet,

sniper-shot through the head at the second Battle
of the Marne—that's how quickly it happens.

Say *love* and death kicks in the door, ejecting spent shells
as it reloads; *click, click.* My old boyfriend's not dead,

but his brother, who parked by the bridge with Susan
St. Clair, is. Five years of Lou Gehrig's Disease,

that's how slowly it happens. Love walks down the road
and death waits at the river. Love wakes in the morning

and death's in a car and you're in the crosswalk,
your mind on a bridge and a boy and a slow moving river

thinking how poems of praise should be about love
and it's Luck that pulls you back, Luck and Split Second Timing,

those two with their lassoes of *not yet, not yet.* Say *love*
and death checks the chamber. Say *death* and love

drops his head in his hands. Say *luck* and bow deeply
to Split Second Timing, since you are alive to read this.

first appeared in *Smartish Pace*

The One and The Other

The child hums as he carries, too late,
his grandmother's sugar-dusted lemon-glazed cake

down the street to the neighbor who needs to be cheered,
too late for the neighbor

who's stepped into the air
of her silent front hall from a ladder-backed chair

her church dress just pressed, her head in a loop she tied
into the clothesline, too late

he unlatches the gate,
walks up the brick walk on his tiptoes, avoiding the cracks

toward the door she unlocked, left ajar, who knows why
or for whom, if on purpose

or not, but because he's too late
she's gone still when he reaches the door and because

he's too late, as he calls out and looks, brilliant sun
burns through haze

pours through sidelights and bevels
through chandelier prisms, strikes white sparks and purples

on ceiling and walls, on the overturned chair, on her stockings
her brown and white

spectator shoes on the floor
and because he's too late he remembers both terror and beauty

but not which came first. But enough of the one
that he ran

and enough of the other
to carefully lay down the cake at her feet.

Rattle #36 (Rattle Poetry Prize)

Hayden Saunier is the author of four books of poetry and one chapbook; her newest collection, *A Cartography of Home,* was published in 2021 by Terrapin Books. Her work has been awarded the Pablo Neruda Prize, Rattle Poetry Prize, Gell Poetry Award, Keystone Prize, and has been published a variety of journals including *VQR, Beloit Poetry Review, Pedestal, Poet Lore, 32 Poems* and *Tar River Poetry*, online at *Poetry Daily, Verse Daily,* and read numerous times by Garrison Keillor for *The Writer's Almanac*. Hayden is also an actor and the founder/director of No River Twice, an interactive multivocal improvised poetry reading and performance. She is proud to be a poet laureate emeritus of Bucks County, Pennsylvania. More at www.haydensaunier.com.

Annie Petrie Sauter

Colorado Beat Poet Laureate 2017-2019

If you wade in the water

when you wade in the water
it is no secret
 That when I drive by
 Certain hidden spots in
 The river
 That I think of you
 That I remember the warm of the boozy feel of handing
 You our bucket
 Full of ordinary treasure
Hand to hand , knee to equally
 Crippled knee
 We passed those plastic hosts up
 Those banks with a meaning
 We constructed for a drunken
 Evening
Disguised
 As purpose .
On purpose
 I would love to watch you wade
 Out into the cold current - as if you
                              Were
A man for a moment
 My man , and then watch as the
 Water filled your waders

Leaving only your idiot smile above
 The river's truth — as it pulled you down .
Past the Almont bridge where we
 Once had walked touching , in what had passed
 For love, Down to
 Gunnison
 Where
Unlike me, They would know
 What to do

With your cold blue body .
Quickly . They would
 Check your pockets
--For anything they could steal
Fast-- and without feeling
They would remove your heart
Before the equally blank cops
Arrived to remove your face
From the face of the earth

Annie Petrie Sauter is a poet of the loud and rowdy variety. She has been published in multiple journals, collections, magazines and underground press publications over the years. She has also had her work published by Berkeley Women's Collective, Bright Hill Press, Great Weather for Media Press, Maverick Press, and the Alternative New Years Day Collection, Poetrybay, and in Reality Beach .Her Book A Plastic Bag of Red Cells was published by Bright Hill Press.

Robert Savino

Suffolk County, New York Poet Laureate 2015-2017
Bards Laureate 2019-2021

Lifechanger

-for Allen Planz

Years after studying Whitman, the most
influential poet and father of free verse,
something shocked the spirit inside its shell,
linking seams with transcendental thread..

Perhaps poetry, with its trigger
on conceptual minds would satisfy
cravings beyond this abstract development,
build a bridge of natural expression.

I sat opposite the teacher, a different teacher,
a fisherman; but this was no ordinary angler.
This was the Captain of Paumanok's briny deep,
setting his depth sensor to exact levels of my experience.

His feedback was a chilling echo of dashed hope,
but I learned to cast a line from him.
The fisherman angled my ambition,
a lesson I've not forgotten like fish forget.

Today, he remains a spirit of encouragement,
peeking through holes in the sky

while fish swim into the tidal wilderness,
far beyond where fog gathers.

Here where he again can say,
"Light is always ahead of the season."

Yen for Yesterday

Soaking rains soften soil where winds
threaten tomatoes holding onto high stakes
out of reach for squirrels with healthy appetites
before acorns fall to a hibernation hunt.

The angry air has abundant space to spread
its deep odorless breath, invisible, without
conscience, in the same space the innocent
yearn to inhale the fresh fragrance of flowers.

And there's only a few out to celebrate the face
of sunshine or to share in the success
of a bountiful harvest.
Happiness is isolated within walls of restriction
where flexibility stretches with little reach.

Voices barely heard in muffled gasps of breath.
Others crying in deafening attempts to live,
cross paths with songbird sparrows . . .
                 everything
hanging onto threads of weak connections.

Robert Savino, Suffolk County Poet Laureate 2015-2017 & Bards Laureate 2019-2021, is a native Long Island poet, Board Member at the Walt Whitman Birthplace and winner of the 2008 Oberon Poetry Prize. Robert is the co-editor of two bilingual collections of Italian Americans Poets (*No Distance Between Us & No Distance Between Us - The Next Collection*). His books include *fireballs of an illuminated scarecrow, Inside a Turtle Shell* and *I'm Not the Only One Here.*

Robert Scott

Prince William County, Virginia, Poet Laureate 2014 - 2016

Cloudbursts

I wish to be young again,

just you and me,

twenty seven and impervious to the immutable clutch of gravity and time.

You, because you deserve it,

me, because I want another chance.

I've got a fistful of carnival tickets, jonesing for a go at that tilt-a-whirl or a

dip into the lunatic delirium of our boardwalk funhouse.

I'll bring a compass this time; I promise.

The algorithm's scribbled on a drunken noodles receipt.

You'll see.

And that's all;

that's the end of the poem.

The rest is a ceramic knickknack we can shatter with a hammer.

***

***

Around 3:15 a.m.

Hope and Regret battle on the distended hummock of my middle-aged belly, smooth in the dark beneath Bed, Bath, and Beyond blankets,

like a freshly-filled grave.

Most nights, I watch.

Regret wears armor plated with ten-thousand lies, failures, missed opportunities, and uncompromising fears. She wields fifty years of boneheaded decisions like Jason Voorhees's machete.

Yet Hope is a determined, nineteen-year-old girl with the loose, blithe endurance of an ultramarathoner.

Back and forth, they clash

until 4:30, when I rouse and wander into another artificially-vanilla-scented day, my soft khaki pockets filled with thumbtacks.

Robert Scott dreams of running all the way across South Dakota, but tragically, he's only given 3 days of personal leave each year - and he's deathly afraid of snakes. He's been a public school teacher for nearly 30 years, so he's grown accustomed to the daily dance of encouraging students to trade their iPhones for a story or two from Edgar Poe. He can play Bach and Mozart on the guitar but most days wishes he could remember the math equations he mastered as a high school kid in 1983. He's utterly addicted to coffee, murder mysteries, and cross country running. If you're around the Manassas Battlefield at 5:30 a.m., feel free to join him for a few miles.

+

Betsy Sholl

Poet Laureate of Maine 2006 - 2011

Shore Walk with Monk

Whoever lived here is gone, but a slick
staircase remains in the broken shell,
damaged just enough to suggest secret
recesses spiraled inside where *something*
slid down to poke out its head,

and when a threat appeared, scurried
or oozed back along those pearly halls.
Someone stood catatonic when shaken down
by cops, but when he felt safe on the bandstand
he'd step out and dance, flap his elbows

like nubby wings, then back to the keyboard
to pick up his place, foot kicking
the piano's invisible flywheel.
Those were the years everyone changed shape,
painters squinted, poked their heads outside the frame.

Why have frames at all—or canvas, or paint?
And why not play the least expected note
so the music's a double exposure,
what's there and what isn't superimposed,
a musical house all fretwork and jut,

246

as if any minute the whole structure
might topple. But a house, once you've entered,
nothing four-square will do. You want those
crooked doors, those circular steps ending
in pure misterioso, you need

those rooms suspended over a bay
where sunlight keeps changing tempo and key—
or so I was thinking when my tape started
to chirp like a hip calliope,
and I took it out to see if I could rewind,

finger holding one reel, pencil turning
the other, like one of his visitors
fidgeting while Monk sits wordless for hours
or grinds his teeth. Funny, how he gets me out
of my own head's maze, its slippery hall of mirrors,

when he could go so far inside his own,
nothing moved but his eyes. Or he'd spend days
in constant motion, pacing and spinning
till the turbulence inside finally found
a room with a bed and laid itself down.

Weeks it could take to stumble back out—
which might explain all the doors and tilted
balconies in his musical house,
Magritte windows with their starry skies
painted on glass, while a perilous void

expanded inside. I'm off the beach,
beside my car by now, unraveling
a Mobius strip of Monk, Monk billowing

over dune grass and rocks, ringing the car's
antenna, Monk in hundreds of tiny

accordion pleats I couldn't undo
no matter how I try, all spiraling out
of their plastic shell, catching the light, pouring
a kind of broken music the maker's
done with, just slipped out of and left behind.

Alms

Small as a fly bump, the little voice
behind me calling *Miss, Miss,* wanted
a dollar, maybe for food as she said

in that voice of mist, so plaintive
and soft it could have come from inside
my own head, a notch below whisper,
voice of pocket lint, frayed button hole,

voice of God going gnat small. I shivered
and stopped. I looked for the source,
and there it was again, *Miss,* so slight

it wobbled moth-like on air,
up from a bare trash-filled recess
beside the post office steps. Yes,
I gave the dollar. But I had seven

in my wallet, so clearly that voice
wasn't small enough, still someone
else's sorrow, easy to brush off—

till later that night, in bed, I heard it
again, smaller—*miss, miss,* little fly strafe
troubling sleep—not a name at all,
but a failure, a lack, a lost chance.

Betsy Sholl served as Poet Laureate of Maine from 2006 to 2011. Her tenth volume of poetry, *As If a Song Could Save You*, winner of the Four Lakes Prize, will be published by the University of Wisconsin Press in fall of 2022. She teaches in the MFA in Writing Program of Vermont College of Fine Arts and lives in Portland, Maine.

Virginia Shreve

<u>Connecticut Beat Poet Laureate, 2020-2022</u>

Philosophy of Thirteen
No Waiting, No Blackbirds

I.

Sometimes, if you are smaller
Weaker, slower
You just got to own a bigger crazy

II.

It is seldom advantageous
To impersonate
An expiring wildebeest

III.

We will never have Paris.
Your Chinese girlfriend threw walnuts at you.
I was secretly married to a man in Texas

IV.

If your dog wants to roll in you
It may be time
For some serious personal grooming

V.

Do not trust a man who says Believe Me
Do not marry a man
Who eats the last brownie

VI.

It is wise not to antagonize crows.
They remember your face
And know which car is yours

VII.

When winter sky is that deep clenching blue
Almost violet
It is nearly enough to make you forsake red

VIII.

You may find yourself groping a married sergeant
In a taxi in Budapest
Or you may not. Life is uncertain. Sometimes sweaty

IX.

Not everyone can taste
Colors
Or swallow music like air

X.

I will not tell you how to mourn.
Sometimes it is weeping. Sometimes it is cake.
Sometimes becoming yourself inside out

XI.

Yodeling is not a mating call
Thank God for chocolate
And strong drink

XII.

Do not pity those who make a madman king.
Better not to give them torches, though
Fiddles maybe

XIII.

Any day you wake up
Not tied in a sack with weasels
Is a good day

Dear Roberta

Why I haven't written in so long

Your cat tried to kill me, you know,
my pulse like a fluttering moth
in my throat, you said

I drank your mother's weak coffee
picking the grounds out of my teeth
She drove to the vet
I carried Mitty in a box
I didn't gloat

Was your mother a bareback rider in the circus?
She looked like she could wear
a plumed headdress
She looked like she knew secrets.
Mine knew more.

The ceiling collapsed
toilets exploded, tires blew, furnace quit
pretending

My father is himself
only part-time now.
He pastes my mother's old face
on the scantily clad bodies of pin-ups

"Unfortunately," began my horoscope
I didn't read the rest
buzzards nested on the roof

We crossed Moon River
mudflats slicked silver and stunk
took the Diamond Parkway into Savannah
for the last time
He didn't look back

Joey and Louis grew up
Louis became a monster
planted hair plugs
whitened his teeth
sharpened them

I know about the dildo in the bedside table
I told him
or meant to
but didn't want to hear the explanation

Alice, unrepentant
Alice slept with a married man

I watched them put the paddles on
Should we get her out of the room they asked
I watched them shock his heart
His body twitched and leaped like it was
escaping

There are claw marks in the vestibule

The bitch was in heat
the dog mad for her

For nine months I felt the swelling
knew the heartbeat
I dream of her tiny pale fingers
like anemones strumming the current

Dear Roberta
I hope the family
is well
dear

Virginia Shreve, grateful to be named the Connecticut Beat Poet Laureate for 2020-2022, considers the honor to be a vast step up from penning a catalogue devoted solely to corrugated office products, as she did in her sordid past. But that was when she lived in Dallas, and she couldn't help herself. After touching down in Kankakee, Siesta Key, Budapest, and other way stations, she now resides in a small river town in CT with husband and dogs, none well-trained, but all good-natured. For years she wrote and edited numerous regional newsletters, much dog humor, and her poems have appeared in print and online in *The Southern Poetry Review, Naugatuck River Review, Slippery Elm, Phantom Drift, Cedar Rock, Crucible, Your Daily Poem,* and others, including various anthologies. Her poem "Tintype" was nominated for a Pushcart Prize.

Ron Smith

Poet Laureate of Virginia 2014-2016

Oxford, 1975
   for Delores

If we had not gone there, away
from our real lives, gone
to drift along the Cherwell
in a haze of good sherry, recline
on elbows by the Isis
like people in ads,

we wouldn't have seen
those spires blacken against
the sky's vast burn and ribboning,
or leaned together
down the High in the hush
of dinner-time shadows, sleeping,

nearly, between our steps,
the day settling

like influenza along our bones,
or found ourselves at twilight
behind the flutist
in his tattered gown
drawing us into Longwall

257

with, yes, "Scarborough Fair,"
black gown floating away,
invisible roses trellised
on the faint smell of soot,
that simple melody
pulling itself out of our hearts

like guilt, like sweet confession,
until, at a turning, the rush
of traffic tore something
from the air, and he strolled,
just a student, flute
swinging at the end of his arm

like the spit hung silver in your snapshot
of a boy on Magdalen Bridge,
and we knew, without
speaking, without
leaning apart to see our eyes,
that we loved each other
and that it would never be enough.

[from *Running Again in Hollywood Cemetery* 2nd edition, MadHat Press, 2020.]

Ron Smith, Poet Laureate of Virginia 2014-2016, is the author of *Running Again in Hollywood Cemetery* (chosen by Margaret Atwood as "a close runner-up" for the National Poetry Series Open Competition and now issued in an expanded second edition) and of three books from LSU Press, most recently *Its Ghostly Workshop* and *The Humility of the Brutes*.

Barbara Southard

Suffolk County, New York, Poet Laureate 2019-2021

Days

The split log cottage I live in is not much more
than a large tree house perched on a hill
surrounded by a curtain of greens in spring
through summer, turning to rusted orange in fall,
then winter trees stripped of all but their graceful
bones, filigreed branches arching over the roof.

Muffled by a stretch of water and hills, I can hear
the ferry horn as it leaves the harbor, and through-
out the day, the soft rumble and whistle of trains
arriving then leaving the station, sounding like
a great friendly beast walking through woods.

Listen, bivalves in the harbor siphon their survival from
water, sending what they don't need back to sea
                                        and did you know
an octopus has three hundred million neurons spread over
the whole of its body in an infinite loop of body and mind.

So many questions still not answered.

Today I will consider the green of the rhododendron,
how light sends out its waves,
how our eyes open wide to receive them.

                              Is this not astonishing?

Watch a baby grow.
She filters her days through mirrors and lenses,
soon learns she is not the center of the universe.

Earlier I was stung by angry wasps protecting their nest by the pond
and the deer have bitten off the daisy buds.

                              Let them have their way.

Dear Whale

There was a time when you were not much
larger than a dog, and like a dog,
walked on land.
No one knows why you abandoned land
for water but I see the attraction.

Some of you have teeth, others silken
curtains that sift your food.
You've learned to blow bubbles to corral your meal,
your songs heard for hundreds of miles.

There was a day when a pod of you
surrounded my son's small fishing boat
off the Lost Coast. You gave him joy
and for that I'll always be in your debt.

After his ashes joined you in the ocean
I saw one of you breach the waters
off the Kenai Peninsula and I thought
I was seeing God—
he was there with you in all your evolved beauty.

Barbara Southard currently serves as Poet Laureate of Suffolk County, New York. One of the projects she's involved in is working with the Long Island Poetry Collective to provide Zoom poetry workshops for those who have lost their workshops during Covid. Special thanks should be given to Richard Bronson, Kate Boning Dickson and Tony Policano for their hard work in hosting and facilitating the workshops. She's also part of a team that holds poetry readings (through Zoom presently) called Second Saturdays. Thanks should also be given to Kathy Donnelly and Dan Kerr for their dedication and service to the community. Barbara Southard's work has been published nationally and internationally in a variety of literary journals and anthologies. She is the author of *Remember,* published in 2008 by Allbook books, and *Time & Space,* published in 2020 by Allbook books.

William Sovern

Indiana Beat Poet Laureate, 2019-2021

New Years Eve

"I keep trying to find out what it really means to be American"
  - Patty Smith

I'm spending New Years
Eve in a blue collar Indiana
town in the pool room of a
Karaoke bar with the spirit of
Isadore Duncan
I drink she dances
I drink she dances
I drink she dances
but it isn't
Isadore Duncan rather a 24
Year old Venus in blue jeans
Somehow I was supposed
to be in New York City down
on Bowery Street eating poetry
for breakfast lunch & dinner
but I'm spending
New Years Eve in the
pool room of a karaoke
bar channeling Woody
Guthrie I would rather be
channeling Alan Ginsberg

But there is no poetry on
the karaoke play list
I'm sitting at a table
in the pool room of
a karaoke bar with
the sons & daughters
of American and it's
midnight and I'm
dressed like Carmen
Maraca and the sons
& daughters of America are
blowing their horns
blowing their horns
blowing their horns
I'm spending New Years
Eve in the pool room of a karaoke
bar in blue collar Indians town

William Sovern hosted poetry performances for 26 years. He has promoted
over 200+ poetry readings in the Evansville, Indiana area. Dr. Santosh Kumar
Describes Sovern's poetic technique as marked by innovation and experimen-
tation. His poems reveal 'hard, dry image', instead of vague, facile and hollow
style of the Georgian poets of the early 20th century. Consequently, Sovern
succeeds in creating poems full of sharpness and preciseness.

Kim Stafford

Oregon Poet Laureate, Emeritus

Lost & Found People

That's what Jamie called them,
when we met in prison
and he spoke of love: "There was
this great big woman," he said —
"big heart, trouble getting around,
so I helped her, we went to all
the homeless camps to round up
the First people, the Native people,
the Lost and Found people, got them
on this bus to the Sun Dance where
you have to bleed to make it
real, to let the Creator see you,
just look up into the sky, into
the sun, let go all the bad you've done,
stand on the ground, on the earth,
open your heart to who you are —
lost and found, lost and found,
I was lost and I was found."

Then Jamie was silent for a time.
There was a light around him
where he sat in that flimsy prison chair.
That light came from the woman he helped.
It came from the sun.

It came from his heart
first hurt when he was young.
It came from what he still has to do.
He carried that light. I carry it.
I give his light to you.

Poetry in Prison

You're in, but the question is:
What's in you? What story
aching to be told do you hold
in solitary, shackled, denied
its rights to visitors?

The hard things that happened are gold
you hammer into shape, the pain
you twist, the grief you make shimmer,
the lost good thing you restore
by telling it back into being.

Everyone is in prison, one way
or another. And everyone is
free, one way or another. The trick
is to find your way to bear the story
forth, so it shines in a listener's eyes.

Kim Stafford, founding director of the Northwest Writing Institute at Lewis & Clark College, is the author of a dozen books of poetry and prose, including *The Muses Among Us: Eloquent Listening and Other Pleasures of the Writer's Craft* and *100 Tricks Every Boy Can Do: How My Brother Disappeared*. His most recent book is the poetry collection *Singer Come from Afar* (Red Hen, 2021). He has taught writing in dozens of schools and community centers, and in Scotland, Italy, Mexico, and Bhutan. In May 2018 he was named Oregon's 9th Poet Laureate by Governor Kate Brown for a two-year term.

Sofia M. Starnes

Virginia Poet Laureate, 2012 - 2014

Archetypes

They never were, they always are—
these children who run heaven in our midst,
who populate our parks,
who lose their daily grit on graveyard walks
but find it in the gravel of their shoes.
We are far stronger than you are, they think;
We are alive and you are not.

I never met them, but I always knew
the tawny moths that fevered on their cheeks.

You've heard me say "Elena" for a girl,
and "Carlos" for the anonymous young boy;
they run home, so the rule says,
when it rains,
they rush off, so my eyes fear, when it storms.
They play, unpausing, with the village brood,
where children seem less clear, less separate—

I never met them, but I always knew
about the notes their oyster-pockets hold.

What do they say?

How do they pick the words?
I'm sure that Carlos clamors his in haste—
he, of the archetypal kind,
who'll lift a sword without excessive qualm,
but who remains a child before the dark.

When shall I draw them out, free from the woods,
he and Elena, and others, fresh from myth?
When will their muddy feet, heard two by two,
turn to the open air of Burnley?
That day, they'll cease their darting in and out,
and come in pairs (or halves) as humans do—

They live in houses, light their fires, and dream
about the world, how it will come to be.

(*The Consequence of Moonlight*, Paraclete Press, 2018;
first published on the National League of American Pen Women website.)

Between

—a dizain sequence

1

A little boy, whose curly hair is gone;
the father's massive head, stubby chin, rough
pallor. He watches, wishing he were stone-
blind to this subtle shell. Less is enough.
Yet, nothing tears his eyes away. His wife
is altar for their quiet son; her skin,
its linen. With a hand, she shadows the thin
sheet, cloudlike. Until the evening carries
him away—this little boy—gradually, in-
to a hush-hush place, where no one hurries.

2

I'm telling you this without having seen
them.   A divide, like the eyelid of a child,
keeps us apart—nightfall over a green
meadow, some children running after wild
geese, others nesting with lambs. Who's exiled?
Who's closer to home? Who murmurs about
a battle fought in the furthermost redoubt?
Who's on the backyard swing? Still, pacing is
our common language: we pace between doubt
and assurance, between hunger and kiss.

3

Some children are never hurrying home;
this much we know from the ephemera
around us, or from the yield of a rhizome,
lifeless between thumbs. Amid a para-
phernalia of things—the end of an era—

270

come our shared bones shouldering a defeat.
Daylight hurts and daylight binds us; all week
the crescent moon rivals the evening star
in our minds, until we hear the wind speak:
Ribs of My ribs, O child of My soul, come far.

Sofia M. Starnes served as Virginia Poet Laureate from 2012 to 2014. She is the author of six poetry collections, most recently *The Consequence of Moonlight* (Paraclete Press, 2018). She is also the recipient of a Poetry Fellowship from the Virginia Commission for the Arts, among other commendations, including the Rainer Maria Rilke Poetry Prize, the *Marlboro Review* Poetry Prize, the Whitebird Poetry Series Prize, five Pushcart Prize nominations, and an honorary Doctor of Letters degree from Union College, Kentucky. Sofia is currently Poetry Editor of the *Virginia Writers Club Journal*. In addition, she is working on a collection of dizains, a 16th century poetry form, which she is recasting in contemporary voice. Some of her recent work appears in *First Things, The Bellevue Literary Review, Notre Dame Review, William & Mary Review, Southern Poetry Review, Presence,* and *Modern Age.* She lives in Williamsburg, Virginia, with her husband, Bill, an emeritus professor of chemistry and jazz pianist. More information about Sofia's work can be found in www.sofiamstarnes.com.

Shelby Stephenson

North Carolina Poet Laureate, 2015-2018

Elvis

Thinking of words that would salvage him, wiggling
Before the microphone, 1954,
Raleigh Memorial Auditorium, my rolled-up sleeves,
Peg-legged pants a camel-turd brown – glory

Be rock-n-roll in the highest,
I was there, chauffeured by my brother Paul,
To see Ferlin Husky, the biggest
Name in country music after Hank, "That's all,"

He said, singing his final song, "I Feel Better All Over More Than Anywhere
Else."
The seats in the auditorium clanked in tunes
Fine, full, perfect as Paul and I
Scampered toward our car for the run

To Paul's Hill, Elvis's face already in the microphone,
"I got a woman, way cross town, she's good to me, yeah!"
Seat-bottoms went down like
The clatter of a train on a track piled with telephones.

"Here, here, here," he comes again,
His white suit shaking, guitar dressed
In something like a baby's bunting.

I was fifteen: I felt the blessed

Show I was witnessing, that haste of stardom
The close-up of fame becoming art,
The blast of records he made, bruising boredom,
With Sam Phillips at Sun, the center of the earth.

In a week or two Elvis Presley was on RCA.
The song, well, we know it, "Heartbreak Hotel,"
The ready throttle of his voice fully packed with grace,
With that extra salute to guts and secrets of nature.

I love to sing country music; yet I never sang
An Elvis song, for once he did it, it was done.
Impersonators come and go, dressed for flim-flam
And money to put in the bank and some for RCA and Sun.

Shelby Stephenson served as Poet Laureate of North Carolina from 2015-2018. Recent books: *Possum* (Bright Hill Press), winner of Brockman-Campbell Award; *Elegies for Small Game* (Press 53), winner of Roanoke-Chowan Award; *Family Matters: Homage to July, the Slave Girl* (Bellday Books), the Bellday Prize; *Paul's Hill: Homage to Whitman* (Sir Walter Press); *Our World* (Press 53); *Fiddledeedee* (The Bunny and the Crocodile Press; reprinted by Press 53); *Nin's Poem* (St. Andrews University Press); *Slavery and Freedom on Paul's Hill* (Press 53); *More* (Redhawk Publications); *Shelby's Lady: The Hog Poems* (Fernwood Press). A member of the Society of Distinguished Alumni, Department of English, University of Wisconsin-Madison, he is Professor Emeritus, University of North Carolina-Pembroke, serving as editor of *Pembroke Magazine* from 1979 until his retirement in 2010. He lives at the homeplace on Paul's Hill, where he was born, near McGee's Crossroads, about ten miles northwest of Benson, North Carolina.

Ed Stever

Suffolk County, New York, Poet Laureate 2011-2013
Bards Laureate 2015-2017

The Boy On The Bridge

The rising river

Is

always here
and it

is

always gone
as I stand contemplating
how close the word
reappear

is

to *reaper.*
And the boy on the bridge
tugs at my trousers
and says, "Hey, mister,
you have tall skin."

And as he dashes

away
I realize
I have not died enough
yet to know anything
greater than the froth
that sloshes
above my shoes.

Poet, playwright, actor, and director, Ed Stever has published two collections of poetry with Writers Ink Press: *Transparency* and *Propulsion*. He has published extensively since 1986 and has garnered numerous writing awards,including a National League of American Pen Women's award. In 2000, he took top prize in Theatre Oxford's Ten Minute Play Competition for *Shakespeare, Time Warps & Black Holes*. As an actor, he has appeared in 34 plays and has also directed numerous productions of his own work and that of others. Ed was adjunct professor at Suffolk County Community College, where he taught Creative Writing, among other courses. He was Suffolk County, NY, Poet Laureate, 2011- 2013 and Bards Laureate 2015-2017.

Priscilla Celina Suarez

McAllen, Texas Poet Laureate 2015-2017

Her Story is my Heirloom

Las comadres in my life,
their stories never wait their turn.
They come in the form of
a tia, a cousin, a colleague, a friend
      and carry
a trace, a bloodline, an inheritance
an atlas
of the worlds before me.

"Ay, comadre, but you are never alone,"
they whisper
and dab at the silences
with a *bidi bidi bom bom*
y se emocionan, ya no razonan
los consejos de quien bien te quiere.

The paths they have taken
come back as cuentos
of those *ooo-oo-ooo, baby, baby* tunes.
Mami's childhood an image in my mind
tell-telling a map of where
      the baby boomers in my family have been.

the stories of las comadres are to be buried

but never hidden
away in the grating lumber chest
my grandparents
brought home from Reynosa. not every moment
has to be so hard
on us
        when the distance
        we travelled
is never far enough
to hide and cry
for fear of belonging...too much to too many.

their stories are rather the worst kind
insisting they have a chance
to exist and re-exist
as they travel
        from one ear out one mouth and into another ear.
so, they become
a rather fragile
heirloom needing constant care
and renovations
        from the passing and re-enacting
an aunt, a cousin, a son, a nephew
bring to light
with the recollection another story
has triggered.

their stories are like a trance
we as offspring cannot escape,
whether because we respect our elders
when they tell us a boring chronicle
of childhoods spent out in the labores
        or because we are enchanted

           by the ghosts
           of an old farmhouse in North Dakota.
experiences which are curative
against blemished ambitions
           and gently ignored
           by our young ignorance
           of appreciating, but not really knowing
what we ourselves
have never encountered.

their stories are fractures
in our ribs
as we slowly breathe out
the subsistence of our departed
           sangre de sangre
           who come out
rolling the punches
and remembering the relampagos
of their earthly existence,
slowly invading
space only the living
are given credit for.
           que en paz descansen
pero
           in another cuento,
we resurrect them
from a tomb of hidden memories
           that are passed on and on and on
           because without them
           our heirloom, our family
           vanishes
into a steady stream of wondering.

Priscilla Celina Suárez is a cofounder of the Gloria Anzaldua Legacy Project and the 2015-17 McAllen Poet Laureate, where she had an opportunity to rediscover the many communities in the Rio Grande Valley. During her childhood, she lived surrounded by the farmlands of the then small colonia of Las Milpas, TX, where she first heard many of the cuentos she shares in her work. A recipient of the *Mexicasa Writing Fellowship*, her poetry is a hybrid of rancheras, polkas, pop, rock, and música internacional. A past contributor to the American Library Association's *Young Adult Library Services* magazine, she authored the Texas State Library's *Bilingual Programs Chapter* – allowing her an opportunity to gain experience in writing poetry, rhymes, and tongue twisters for children and teens. She has shared her poetry in *¡Juventud!: Growing up on the Border* and *Along the River III: Dark Voices from the Río Grande*. In 2003, her work was selected by The Monitor as *The Best Poetry of the Year*.

Gayl Teller

Nassau County, New York Poet Laureate 2009-2011

At the Immersive Van Gogh Exhibit

While one visitor sees Van Gogh's self-portrait
on a vast wall, upside down,
sinking into the sea as a sunset,

another sees that face reflected on the floor,
right side up, rising from the water
as a well-fed seabird,

and another sees those eyes sliding
across a visitor's chest as she moves
across a glass globe in reflection,

while another sees her own eyes
mirrored back from a glass prism tower
as her eyes merge with Van Gogh's—

maybe Van Gogh, too, had a different experience
each time he looked at one of his portraits,
incompleting the painting each time he looked—

as those masked, sitting in socially distanced
pandemic circles, see this moving portrait uniquely,
whether they're lying down, leaning left or right,

whether turning their heads, or on their heels,
whether watching the fractured features as the face
projects across a jagged, reflective sculpture,

or carrying that fractured face away on themselves,
unawares, on their own body surfaces,
in this shifting kaleidoscope of Van Gogh brush strokes

actively painting across every surface of 3 vast rooms,
across the floors, across the walls, across the ceilings,
as each room opens into each other's changing vistas,

brush strokes creating and recreating his irises as they bloom,
his sunflowers as they enclose me, my hmmm
hmmming like a buzzing bee's on the sweets,

and visitors are bending with his potato eaters,
sitting with his card players, stretching up
into his cypress trees, winging over

rippling red-green waters with his birds,
as the arches of the Arles asylum, where
he was committed as fractured, go swimming

in multiple directions all around the room,
and the floor is rising in shimmering rivulets
with music embedded in the vibrant colors,

then falling into the starry night cosmos swirling
all around no absolute perspective,
as old faces are melting into young faces,

into dazzling hues in creation's fluid universe,
where visitors are turning into paintings,
entering the fidelity of otherworldly dimensions,

where paintings are all process in motion,
and visitors are all painters with their own
moving perspectives, shifting realities,

and millions keep participating across the US,
across Italy, across Brussels, across the UK,
with the man who died penniless, obscure,

because being alive means eyes need to brush
with branches of light and resounding colors
so they might sing in art's glorious hills.

Off to Work

As small as Rahul is, for he's only six,
and so far away from me he shrinks
in the distant Tumakuru dawn,
as he carries his filthy plastic bag
his mother bestowed, sent him off again
unmasked, barefoot, with his bump
of malnourished belly,
as I relish another spoonful of rainbow cake,
tartufo on top, mask in my pocket,
at the diner's outdoor table, six feet from others,
and Rahul rummages through a garbage dump
littered with broken glass, slits his thumb,
as he lifts a shard from among stinky discards,
prizes the plastic piece to recycle
for his mother, for a few cents per hour
since March, when India closed its schools,
and no one has praised him as "bright"
as his teacher had since then,
as I, on leave since the pandemic,
unknowing how to teach online for real,
pay the check to the masked waiter, drive off
with Rahul facing up, lying next to me,
his eyes open and bound by where I take them
as they look out from the front page,
but Rahul and I will never meet
the further, the faster I drive away
in my distant galaxy of experiences,
yet the more he shrinks from my sensibility,
the dimmer each step he takes in my view

with his bleeding unshod soles,
his stabbing hungry belly,
the larger Rahul gets in the looming
entangled human family.

~ "At the Immersive Van Gogh Exhibit" (*The Seventh Quarry, Swansea Poetry Magazine"*
~ "Off to Work" (*Corona, An Anthology of Poems*-- Walt Whitman Birthplace Association, 2020)

Nassau County, NY, Poet Laureate for 2009-11 and the Walt Whitman Birthplace 2016 Poet of the Year, Gayl Teller is author of 7 poetry collections, most recently, *Flashlight: New and Selected Poems* (WordTech/ Cherry Grove Collections, 2019) and the editor of two poetry anthologies— *Toward Forgiveness* (Writers Ink, 2011): awarded a NY State Decentralization Grant for the Arts, and *Corona: An Anthology of Poems* (Walt Whitman Birthplace Association, 2020). Director of the Poetry Series at the Mid-Island Y, in Plainview, NY, and a Hofstra University professor, she has been the recipient of many national and international poetry awards. Her website: www.gaylteller.com

Larry D. Thomas

Texas Poet Laureate, 2008

A Few Months Shy of Ninety
(Far West Texas)

She lives alone in an old stone
house on the outskirts of Alpine.

Though her petite frame's acquiesced
a tad to the nagging lists

of arthritis, her mind's quite keen,
active as an uncaged cactus wren.

To honor her dead husband,
she's declined at least a dozen

blue-rivered hands offered her
in marriage. A list of widowers

lies folded in her bedside table
drawer, each willing and able

to lead her in a wicked Texas
Two-Step culminating in safe affection,

sans the baggage of attachment,
just enough to keep her cheeks sanguine

and her arteries free of fat.
Too old to fret, she likes it like that.

(first published in *New Texas*)

Larry D. Thomas, a member of the Texas Institute of Letters and the 2008 Texas Poet Laureate, has published twenty-three print books of poetry and numerous online chapbooks. He resides in the Chihuahuan Desert of south-western New Mexico. His Web site is www.larrydthomas.com

Mary Langer Thompson

**Senior Poet Laureate, California 2012**

Poem in Water

By Lingering Lake
I watch a Chinese poet
with sweeping brush strokes
write characters
in water
upon the pavement.

Disciples follow in silence
under the willow trees
reading retextured liquid,
the path an impermanent context.

I can't decipher the message
of this groundling poem,
but feel unmoored
then embraced, bent and baptized,
evaporating verse
washing the dust from my heart.

Cell Phones and Song Cells

Usually, I like
to drive and sing
with the radio.
But not today.
I'm racing across freeways
to join you in
an emergency room.

I read that
canaries stop singing
each autumn
when their song-generating
neurons die.

You were able to tell me,
with slurred speech
over the carphone that
your head felt strange,
you were too dizzy
to walk.

In winter, the birds' neurons
grow back. In spring
they learn their songs
all over again.

I step harder on the gas,
knowing that
if you leave me,
replenished neurons or not,
I will not sing.

Dr. Mary Langer Thompson's articles, short stories, and poetry appear in various journals and anthologies. She is a contributor to Women and Poetry: Tips on Writing, Teaching and Publishing by Successful Women Poets (McFarland) and was the 2012 Senior Poet Laureate of California. A retired principal and English teacher, she now writes full time in Apple Valley, California where she received the Jack London Award in 2019 from the High Desert Branch of the California Writers Club.

Tammi Truax

Portsmouth, New Hampshire Poet Laureate 2019-2021
Maine Beat Poet Laureate 2018-2020

For Lonesome George, the last Pinta Island Tortoise

On reading *The Last of its Kind* (The Atlantic, June 2019) by Ed Yong

The last, the very last
one of a species
is called an endling.
When the last
one of a species
dies, disappears
it usually goes unnoticed
by us. But always
it leaves behind a body;
The ending of an endling.

When there is
but one left
the species is already,
of course, extinct.
The endling then
is just surfing solo
in its lonely little place
on the sixth mass wave,
representing, giving us,

spectators on the messy beach
a chance, a last chance,
to say good-bye,
or sorry, or something,

instead of sticking our heads
in the sand to hide from
the truth and the heat
of the scorching sun
we installed in the
perfect sky.

Tammi Truax, an MEd graduate of Plymouth State University, is a writer, teacher and school librarian. Her poetry has appeared in twelve anthologies, including *The Widows' Handbook: Poetic Reflections on Grief and Survival* with a foreword by Justice Ginsburg (Kent State University Press, 2014). A YA verse novel, *For to See the Elephant* (Piscataqua Press), was released in 2019 and a volume of poetry in 2022. She has prose in *Compass Points* (Piscataqua Press, 2015) and *The Mud Chronicles: A New England Anthology* (Monadnock Writer's Group, 2018). Her work can be found in several journals, newspapers, magazines, and online. Tammi served as the Maine Beat Poet Laureate and the Portsmouth (NH) Poet Laureate with a project that was covered in the New York Times and AP. When not at work she is at home in a Maine cottage making final revisions to a two book historical novel for adults to be published by Oghma Creative Media.

Chris Vannoy

**National Beat Poet Laureate, United States 2019**
**Beat Poet Laureate, California 2017-2019**

His Heart

His heart is a pothole its edges cracked and broken
The center filled with course crushed asphalt and mud
He has no willow in him to let the wind pass through
Just concrete and rock

He scoops handfuls of sand into his mouth then
turns his face upwards and drinks in the cold rain
chews, then swallows
… he eats no dandelion seeds to make him dream
…no vines grow around him to keep him warm

He is wedged between the boulders that Sisyphus has let roll down the hill
tries to stand alone as he yells against a stiff wind
into the silence of his own m i s e r y
that does not care to listen

Chris Vannoy has read up and down both the east and west coast. He was the Beat Poet Laureate of California 2018 and the United States Beat Poet Laureate in 2019. During those years he completed 2 tours of Europe. His first reading in London was at the church where William Blake was baptized and his last reading was in Dylan Thomas's childhood birthplace in Swansea Wales   Last year he was invited to attend the TANTA poetry Festival in Tanta, Egypt. This year he was given the Beat Poet Laureate Lifetime award.

Angie Trudell Vasquez

Madison, Wisconsin Poet Laureate

Kick the Can

Trains rattle across Four Mile Creek
carry livestock to feed the hungry machine.

Swiming in flooded cornfields   we crawl through DDT.

Mulberries purple stain ooze through bare toes,
starburst heels. Mosquitos buzz in our ears –

feed on limbs, bite under shorts. Tics land
on our heads cause night body inspections.

Corn arms scratch our legs as we run through farmers'
young rows play find the scarecrow, the hobo.

We cut off kids play   *kick the can*   under earthshine
cry out in the soft blue dark.

Sweet clover, dandelions, oak trunks
know our names as we dangle –

from stripped limbs   dive off at six feet.
I am nine, the ringleader, the *I know* girl.

We tell ghost stories, hunt for clues, peer into panes

little ones stand on shoulders to see   report back.

We trample earth paths, search for caves,
sunken farm houses, old graves. Sometimes –

semis tip over and hooves clatter up
our dead end street, earth crashing roar

nostril thunder   snorts   steam…
Cows and horses destined for meat packing plants

plot for freedom, pass under our window frames
their last chance hangs.

Mothers run out of their kitchens scoop stunned toddlers
from the middle of the stampede

remark how often this happens   animals
breaking semi steel doors.

Winegardner Road   where underground railroads ran
and good Iowans hid refugees in root cellars

in between fake walls, civil wars
until the next train crossed the land,

the creek, loess fields   straight line from China
spine of tundra. Trains still rattle

carry oil, soybeans.   And children
stub their toes bloody all summer play

kick the can   barefoot on concrete
moisture riding their back, sweat beads

the second they leave the shower. Reporters –
crack eggs on sidewalks the whites steam…

Angie Trudell Vasquez is a poet, writer, performer, and activist. She is the current City of Madison Poet Laureate. Angie Trudell Vasquez received her MFA in poetry from the Institute of American Indian Arts. Her work was recently featured by Tracy K. Smith, former U.S. Poet Laureate, on the poetry podcast, *The Slow Down*, which is broadcast daily on Minnesota Public Radio. Most recently her work has been published in *Taos Journal of Poetry, Yellow Medicine Review, Raven Chronicles, The Rumpus, Cloudthroat,* and the *South Florida Poetry Journal.* She has poems on the Poetry Foundation's website, and was a Ruth Lilly fellow while at Drake University. In 2018 she was a finalist for the New Women's Voices series and her book, *In Light, Always Light,* her third collection of poetry, was published by Finishing Line Press in May 2019. She guest edited the Spring 2019 edition of the *Yellow Medicine Review* with Millissa Kingbird. She is co-editing a collection presently with Margaret Rozga, current Wisconsin Poet Laureate, entitled *Through This Door,* to be released in fall 2020. She serves on the Wisconsin State Poet Laureate Commission as co-chair.

Chryssa Velissariou

Greece Beat Poet Laureate, Lifetime
International Beat Poet Laureate, 2017-2018

Guilt

Your flaming words
like little diamonds,
polyhedral,
engraved gems
at depots in
her darkened mind.

Consolation
of a thirsty
innocent soul
for romantic
passion's heartbeat.
She's hurt by you!

She believed that
they were purchased
in bloodthirsty
hellish deep mines
down in Africa
through skinny hands
of black children,
who were hungry
for altruism's truth.

You had bought them,
man, so cheaply,
in odd bazaars
of illegal,
artificial,
rare gems workshops,
up there in the
liar steppes' cold.

Tiny diamonds,
so resistant,
her dropping tears,
they have washed you
and let you nude
in front of your
own being's needs and,
in the end, squashed,
you have fled in
violent escape.
Your silent scream
unresponsive
to her carnage.

You, through your lies,
ashamed yourself.
And the love which
you felt, was like
flame retardant
grenade, cut
the victim's guts
as bad as yours,
of the addicted

storyteller.

So, well yes, she
will recover...
You have been lost,
just sat upon
a continuous
dream's illusion.

In A Net

Do you feel it, how unbearable is
to be alone
among the crowd?

To be elsewhere,
with mismatched people
who are looking for your love though?

Do you realize you're in a net,
which you set up yourself,
ignoring that you're drowning in it?

Impossible!
You surely know about your own prison...
Many degrees of your freedom
got limited over time.
After that moment you had set up
that ugly success plan.

My little soul,
when did you realize you were going to fly?
Do you feel the foot of time on your chest now?

I managed to reach perfection,
I was lucky,
I existed where I belong
for several moments,
for several charming hours.

Ah, but I feel deep nostalgia for them

and that torch of dearth
is torturing me often silently.

My little soul,
you were born for ethers and
you are in a hurry
to be free sooner ...

What other adjoining souls were you attracted
to that net
where you are entangled?
You are responsible for them!

Hang on the best you can in there,
no matter if your wings flutter.
You owe to your followers!

You cannot leave,
even if you have the chance,
it is not right!
You are not entitled to escape.

Because of these innocent souls
that kept you company all these years
They shouldn't be obliged to pay
the debts you would leave behind...

Chryssa Velissariou, published Poet and Physics professor, and entrepreneur, the 1st International Beat Poet Laureate, Greece 2017-18, Greece Beat Poet Laureate 2019-Lifetime, honored by the National Beat Poetry Foundation, Inc.

Pramila Venkateswaran

Suffolk County, New York Poet Laureate 2013-2015

Young Wonder

These days when the world is in lockdown
I like to walk to the pond, sit on a downed log and watch
flies buzz above rippling water. They must sense
the monster just below the glassy skin. A frog leaps
up and snaps its prey in a trice.

Oak and maple rise serenely all around. Dressed in green
and red, they are grandmothers who've seen the antics
in the pond for years—stupid insects, foolish humans
dipping their sticks in the water to poke at fish, wily foxes
spying the banks, humans who scream beside
the placid water to loosen the knots in their hearts.

"I want to count all the frogs in the pond," a boy tells
his mom. "Like the chimpanzee lady on TV?" asks
the mom. "Yep. Can the frogs hear me? Tell me
what they are saying." "Imagine," says the mom,
so he kneels on the grass and peers into the emerald
depths and sees and hears frogs riding tortoises,
iguanas laughing, fish dining on flies.

Autobiography

I was a ball passed from hand to hand.
"Unbelievable. 9 pounds?" they cooed.
My mother placed a black dot on my cheek
to ward off the evil eye, fed me arrowroot,
and formula, and watched me grow chubbier
than any infant in the neighborhood.
Most of all I fed on strangers' how-cute-
never-seen-such-a-fat-child-from-such-a-thin
woman, as she wheeled me up and down
the city. When my hair grew, my mother
twisted it into two tight plaits and put me
in frilly dresses and set me in the compound
to play hide and go seek. I cried when I could not
find her, and when she appeared with outstretched arms,
I clung to her so tightly, she could not change
out of her sari to go to bed.

Pramila Venkateswaran, poet laureate of Suffolk County, Long Island (2013-15) and co-director of Matwaala: South Asian Diaspora Poetry Festival, is the author of *Thirtha* (Yuganta Press, 2002) *Behind Dark Waters* (Plain View Press, 2008), *Draw Me Inmost* (Stockport Flats, 2009), *Trace* (Finishing Line Press, 2011), *Thirteen Days to Let Go* (Aldrich Press, 2015), *Slow Ripening* (Local Gems, 2016), and *The Singer of Alleppey* (Shanti Arts, 2018). She has performed the poetry internationally, including at the Geraldine R. Dodge Poetry Festival and the Festival Internacional De Poesia De Granada. An award winning poet, she teaches English and Women's Studies at Nassau Community College, New York. Author of numerous essays on poetics as well as creative non-fiction, she is also the 2011 Walt Whitman Birthplace Association Long Island Poet of the Year. She is a founding member of Women Included, a transnational feminist association.

Edward Vidaurre

McAllen, Texas Poet Laureate 2018-2019

When A City Ends

I.
a poor kid sees clean clear water
he envisions a treasure, a hope
have you ever seen a murky
opaque wishing well?

II.
When a woman kneels
along the river's edge to wash her sheets,
she thinks, a new beginning, a cleansing,
when was the last time you washed your clothes in oil?

III.
When a thirsty stray dog walks for miles
along the gutters of this nation
wishing to quench her thirst
where does she find relief?

IV.
When have you seen
dogs or cats, blood dripping
from their jaw hair
laying on your front porch content?

It happens, blood and oil mix with mother earth's tears, and
we watch as it happens.

V.
Soon we'll be drenched.

VI.
question marks fall from trees in place of leaves, a girl yells at me saying her
dog has down syndrome and that I should believe her like I believe in last
night's moon, "even if he does" I cry, I worry about being bitten. When a city
ends, poems get shorter, sometimes just a word long. We stay away from win-
dows, and breathe slowly in anticipation of, what, the end? People loot and
turn mad, while others pull flowers out of the rubble, sometimes finding the
missing not meant to be found. They hear a loud voice coming from the North,
sounds of wailing drums, the sound of a faint condolence, like gasps.

VII.
the earth sneezes, snores, and coughs, and you feel like grabbing the priest
from his collar and demanding an answer. You sleep with jeans and tennis
shoes on in case you need to run out of your home, in the silence of night you
hear the cries and howls and sirens. You hear death. You see nothing. Nor-
malcy is replaced with eeriness and the moon wears down on you something
heavy. You want to sleep, but the earth starts to tremble again. Your past due
bills are forgiven until everything is back to normal, then you return to the
purple of days.

VIII.
I do yard work and get all sweaty. I wait for the smell to set in. I splash some
old spice and I'm the old you. Armpits and cologne. I walk around smiling
and on my tip-e-toes to make myself tall like you, I call out for the cenzontle
that flew away the day you died. I drink coffee and watch black and white

movies. I imagine the woman in my home old and fragile, I tell her to cuss me out, because today I am you, and I'm man enough to take it.

IX.

I buy a stack of postcards with tacuazín having seizures: cure them with short poems, send them to prison inmates doing time for resisting the oligarchies of the world. Boil a beef shank and discard the meat, suck out the marrow while watching a soccer match between Everton and Manchester United. Go up on the roof and count passing cars with low tire pressure and engine trouble. Empty your pockets and put contents in a ziplock bag, if you have a box of cigarettes, smoke two at a time until your tongue gets scratchy, then proceed to lick a cat. Watch the evening news and scream "Lies, Lies, Lies" until the national anthem comes on. Write a lullaby or ode to your neighbor. Drink warm milk. Close your eyes. Count your breaths. Call me in the morning. This is how I cure the insomniac.

X.

my memory returns, I'm twelve again. I am in love with a cinnamon skin colored girl who spends her day washing clothes in a light blue painted pila under a cloudless sky. I write poems to her every night in her native tongue that she can't decipher, so I draw hearts and balloons, stick figure animals and little children holding hands. I don't recall hurricanes or politics at that age, life was better in that third world country. Only the adults died at one time in my life, we just went missing. Music was life, the anthem of my youth was filled with bass drums and the introduction of raging resistance raps, when I couldn't move I listened to 80s love songs. I wrote more love poems, this time to Julia Roberts and Drew Barrymore and Wonder Woman. I was Erik Estrada on a motorcycle, with a gun, without violence, with a big smile, with straight teeth, with a badge that took down the maliantes, with an accent on this side of the border, on a television set, in a make believe world. I fear nothing when my memory returns, my mom is young and dyes her hair a color not to hide greys, but because she still feels beautiful enough to bring out the green in her eyes. I am fifteen again, the earth shakes and I ask God to forgive me for the first time.

Edward Vidaurre is an award-winning poet and author of eight collections of poetry. He is the 2018-2019 City of McAllen, Texas Poet Laureate, 2022 inductee to the Texas Institute of Letters, and publisher of FlowerSong Press. His writings have appeared in The New York Times, The Texas Observer, Los Angeles Review of Books, as well as other journals and anthologies. He has edited over 50 books and anthologies. Vidaurre resides in McAllen, Texas with his wife and daughter.

Daniela Voicu

Romanian Beat Poet Laureate, Lifetime

In every trace remained
a road
in every step
remains a shadow
green is not anymore green only
in the crouced love forgotten in a corner of the room
where
hidden
we sat with masks on face
and with our hands in sight-
our word was stolen
our air and sun were stolen
fear has traveled millions of tiny steps
from
 every edge of the gaze of deserted roads
to the strangest thoughts-
no man
no birds
no sound

"let's hold hands
or to hug?"
is the last movie we saw at the cinema
and all over the planet ...

where is the little girl dressed in red who was
running through the park after a clown
to buy rainbow-balloons?

Daniela Voicu is a Romanian poet and painter. Her poems, interviews,
articles and paintings have been published in various international
journals, magazines and anthologies. Lifetime Romanian Beat Poet
Laureate May 18,2018

James P. Wagner (Ishwa)

National Beat Poet Laureate, United States, 2020-2021
Beat Poet Laureate Long Island, New York 2017-2019

Everyday Alchemy
Alchemy _noun_

1. _the medieval forerunner of chemistry, based on the supposed trans-formation of matter. It was concerned particularly with attempts to convert base metals into gold or to find a universal elixir._

To turn lead, into gold
a power that countless have sought out
through the ages
many of the smartest minds in history had tried
their hand
at this craft, yet hundreds of years of research
and the conclusions of modern chemistry
have taught us
that this science
is a pseudoscience,
alchemy doesn't exist.

And yet, my mind, and eyes, have never fully
received that memo
because I see alchemy every day.
I see it in my cup of coffee
when I think of the magic of the change that these
beans go through, with a little hot water

311

I see it in the kitchen, with every amazing meal
cooked
I see it in the morning paper,
a mere combination of ink and parchment, that now
conveys untold information
through abstract lettering, that we can actually
understand.
I see alchemy performed masterfully through the
kids at the lemonade stand,
taking literally the life gives you lemons quote
and turning it into pocket money
to buy things, that will enhance their summer
creating experiences, and fun times they will
cherish forever.
I see alchemy in the classroom, where the teachers
turn books and lessons
into knowledge
I see it in the roads we take, that have cut our long
journeys down from days or weeks
to minutes or hours
I see it in the inventor, the business owner, the
repairman, the plumber, the carpenter
I hear it, in the music
I see it, on the stage, and the television screen,
I look at it, in the art gallery, and the museum
I see alchemy,
the concept of turning something of little worth
into something of great worth
in almost everything I see around me.
When I really look, with knowing eyes.
Perhaps the scientists and historians who have
declared alchemy
a dead art, have just gotten so used to the magic

so desensitized to the transmutations we perform
on a daily basis
that they forgot to look deeper
and appreciate
everyday alchemy.

Waiting For My Sister

"I'm waiting for my sister,"
I say sometimes
to people who don't know me
see me waiting on the sidewalk outside
of a busy place where people come and go
and me standing by an entrance
could be just another person
waiting for someone
even a sister.
It's always strangers I say this too
not someone who thinks of me
as an only child
who would know
I'm not really waiting
for someone at these places
see, I haven't had a sister in close to 30 years
since the time I sat on my mother's lap
and asked her how long would it be
until the baby came
too young to understand
what premature birth meant
being told only
that she wasn't coming anymore
but even now
nearly 30 years later
 in some ways
I still am
and always will be
waiting for my sister.

George Wallace

National Beat Poet Laureate, United States 2015
Suffolk County, New York Poet Laureate LI NY 2003-2005

Peace Is Honey

Peace isn't the absence of war.
It is sweet milk in a clean bucket.
It is the bleating of goats in an honest
man's yard. Peace is the honking of geese
in the pond, cicadas chirping in the tall grass.
Peace is olive presses, wine presses,
harvesters clamoring for more fruit
in the foothills of the Lower Galilee.
More than silence of dawn with no rockets
to disturb it, peace is rooster crowing,
hen clucking -- plow points, shovels and
stiff rakes and hoes rattling in the back
of a pickup truck. It is the buzz of harvest
machines combing the harmonious land –
horizon to horizon, feeding all the
children women and men without
prejudice, giving all the people
in the land full employ.
Peace is Palestinian boys
in the apiaries of Doura,
west of Hebron, working
their father's hives.It is
a cloud of honeybees

hovering over the roof-
tops of Kibbutz
Ayelet Hashahar.
Peace is not just
the absence of
small arms fire,
or treaty-signing
ceremonies in
far away capitals.
It is more than just
who gets what,
who loses what,
and both sides
agree to accept it.
Peace is more than
the absence of war.

Peace is wild ducks splashing in the Jordan River.
Peace is the shared laughter of workers in the field.

Peace is honey and milk in the land of milk and honey.

Sunday Morning Before The Creation Of The Modern World

By mid-day
the sun
will break through
the river fog
(with its mourn-
ful heart intact)
but for now
a lone seine
worker on the
woeful dock
contemplates
his clay pipe
(on the bank a
man & child of
the middle class
too statuesque for
intimacy stand
safely distant from
each other) -- this is
Sunday morning
before the creation of
the modern world
before the creation of
the modern world
the Bridge at Courbevoie
Seurat at his gray
dismal best
a lingering dolor
like regret
suffuses every
waking soul

317

(not until noon
will the bathers
arrive, with their
picnic baskets and
working class joy) --
what delicate
sensibility
holds sway
(like a gypsy
violin) this is the
hour of the forlorn
this is Milhaud
before he discovered
jazz on the streets
of Harlem (the year was
1923) in this picture
it is 1886
we are gathered
here, bankside
in the midst
of a supreme
dying pastorale
(in the horizon a
smokestack pierces
the unity of
heaven) -- is this
even Sunday? Will
the churchbells
never ring?)

no call
to worship
greater than this --
solitude
in the mist

George Wallace is the first poet laureate of Suffolk County, LI NY (2003-2005), first poet laureate of the Beat Poetry Festival (2008-9), writer in residence at the Walt Whitman Birthplace (2011-present), and author of 37 chapbooks of poetry. A professor of English at Pace University in NYC, he is a major organizer and supporter of poetry communities nationwide, and travels internationally to share his work. He was recently honored with the Alexander Gold Medal for contributions to the arts by UNESCO-Piraeus, Greece, the first American to receive this recognition.

Marjory Wentworth

South Carolina Poet Laureate 2003-2020

Holy City

"Only love can conquer hate."
                    Reverend Clementa Pinckney

Let us gather and be
silent together like stones
glittering in sunlight

so bright it hurts our eyes
emptied of tears and searching
the sky for answers.

Let us be strangers
together as we gather
in circles wherever we meet,

to stand hand in hand and sing
hymns to the heavens and pray
for the fallen and speak their names:

Clementa, Cynthia, Tywanza,
Ethel, Sharonda, Daniel,
Myra, Susie and Depayne.

They are not alone. As bells
in the spires call across
the wounded Charleston sky,

we close our eyes and listen
to the same stillness ringing
in our hearts, holding onto

one another like brothers,
like sisters because we know
wherever there is love, there is God.

Published in *Illuminations,* 31, Summer 2016; *The Post and Courier* June 21, 2015, and BBC NEWS (6 days after the killings at Mother Emanuel Church)

In the Shadows of Nuremberg

For Henry Barbanel

Because we are forever weak
and wounded, looking for someone
to follow or blame; sometimes
we become savage and change
the rules to ease our minds.
Clouded by delusions
of power or fame, human
beings can justify anything.

Too often things can go wrong
in a hurry, and the masses
go along as if their hearts
were turned inside out, and hatred
was something long hidden
but there, like a riptide
pulling below the glittering
smooth surface of the sea.

Abandoning everything
we know is right, we become
tribal and primitive,
tearing the ties that bind us
one to another, as if
they were made of air. And love
dissolves into something
lost in the cruel cacophony.

And though it may be far,

there is always a storm
swirling somewhere. The sea
that connects and creates us,
holds the seeds of our destruction.
Still, God keeps nothing from us.
Each new wave is a renewal;
every day a gift of our own making.

As we stumble from the shadows
of the twentieth century,
covered in blood and ash,
cradling the bones of those who are lost,
we know there can be justice;
the pattern has been set.
No matter how long it takes,
there is no peace without redemption.
Without shadows, there is no light.

Written for the commemoration of the 70th Anniversary of the Closing of the International Military Tribunal at Nuremberg (1946)

Published in: *About Place Journal: Works of Reistance, Resilience* Oct. 2020 and *American Society of International Law,* 2017.

Marjory Wentworth is the *New York Times* bestselling author of *Out of Wonder, Poems Celebrating Poets* (with Kwame Alexander and Chris Colderley). She is the co-writer of *We Are Charleston, Tragedy and Triumph at Mother Emanuel*, with Herb Frazier and Dr. Bernard Powers and *Taking a Stand, The Evolution of Human Rights,* with Juan E. Mendez. She is co-editor with Kwame Dawes of *Seeking, Poetry and Prose inspired by the Art of Jonathan Green,* and the author of the prizewinning children's story *Shackles.* Her books of poetry include *Noticing Eden, Despite Gravity, The Endless Repetition of an Ordinary Miracle* and *New and Selected Poems.* Her poems have been nominated for The Pushcart Prize seven times. She served as the poet laureate of South Carolina from 2003-2020. Wentworth is a 2020 National Coalition Against Censorship Free Speech is for Me Advocate. She teaches courses in writing, poetry, social justice and banned books at The College of Charleston (marjorytwentworth.net).

Ron Whitehead

National Beat Poet Laureate, United States 2021-2022
Beat Poet Laureate, Kentucky 2019-2021

The Underground

More than once
I have been a recluse.
I have lived in the woods,
away from everyone,
studying the Essenes.
Much of my life
has been spent
as a member of The Underground.
I abhor politics.
The politics of greed.
The politics of power.
The politics of raping pillaging murdering
Mother Earth and animals and people
in order to selfishly gain and maintain power.
But abhorring the history of greed,
the history of power,
is only half of my story.
I do not want
what is not mine
is the other half of my story.
Thankfully, not everyone
is an insane greed and maniacal power tyrant.
The only government for me

is the government of individual responsibility
and helping my neighbors.
Have i always been individually responsible?
Of course not.
Have I always helped my neighbors?
Of course not
I have failed more times
than everyone I know put together.
I have said "FUCK OFF!" many times.
But people change. I do.
Change is the number one universal principle.
Though often painful,
I embrace change.
Throughout my life,
I have changed.
There came a point where
I chose to make decisions
that impact my life,
and the lives of others,
in unselfish ways.
I have come to understand
that being individually responsible
and helping my neighbors
creates the healthiest personal,
communal, global environment.
I choose to walk this path
as far as it will go.
I want to see where it will go.
I like not hurting others.
I like being a good neighbor.
I like having friends.
I love people and animals
and all the terrible beauty

that Mother Earth bestows upon us.
I do not want what is not mine.
I always remain
one step away
from being a recluse.
I am happy in the solitude
of inner and outer nature.
I am a member of The Underground.

Poet, writer, editor, publisher, professor, scholar, activist Ron Whitehead is the author of 24 books and 34 albums. In 1994 he wrote the poem "Never Give Up" with His Holiness The Dalai Lama. In 1996 he produced the Official Hunter S. Thompson Tribute featuring Hunter, his mother Virginia, his son Juan, Johnny Depp, Warren Zevon, Douglas Brinkley, David Amram, Roxanne Pulitzer, and many more. Ron has produced thousands of events and festivals, including 24 & 48 & 72 & 90 hour non-stop music & poetry Insomniacthons,in Europe and the USA. He has presented thousands of readings, talks, and performances around the world. He has edited and published hundreds of titles including works by President Jimmy Carter, His Holiness The Dalai Lama, Seamus Heaney, Wendell Berry, Allen Ginsberg, Jack Kerouac, William S. Burroughs, Lawrence Ferlinghetti, Rita Dove, Diane di Prima, Bono, John Updike, Douglas Brinkley, Jim Carroll, Anne Waldman, Joy Harjo, Yoko Ono, Robert Hunter, Amiri Baraka, Hunter S. Thompson, and numerous others. The recipient of many awards, his work has been translated into 20 languages. In 2018 Louisville Mayor Greg Fischer presented Ron with a Lifetime Achievement for Work in The Arts Award. In 2019 Ron was named Kentucky's Beat Poet Laureate and was also the first U.S. citizen to be named UNESCO's Tartu City of Literature Writer-in-Residence. He is co-founder and Chief of Poetics for Gonzofest Louisville. Outlaw Poet: The Legend of Ron Whitehead movie will be released by Storm Generation Films/Dark Star TV in 2021.

Thom Woodruff

Texas Beat Poet Laureate, 2020-2022

The Night Sky
No Body Knows All Of You

Celestial agencies plot the path of orbits
of asteroids with future appointments
Nobel Prizes are given-to those who see and acknowledge
the Black Hole at the center of our existence
We stare Up only sometimes
to see the kiss of moon and stars and planets
but that star map was written long ago
as it moves across the blackness
with temporary illuminations
Larger than our Only Earth
from which we came in birth
and leave and stay and change
While Night Skies remain in play
of Consciousness-wider,taller,deeper
than word or dream or vision
Night Sky horizon to horizon has seen
pre-us,pre-our becoming and our being
Older than gods with names and goddesses anon
Night sky both engineer and witness
Mute only if you do not believe
that stars have consciousness
and it changes us/as the weight of planets
sings through body space.Violent births in forever flames

in time shifts deeper,darker than we can ever see or know
It glows!From our first eye,we tried to name the gods
but they had different destinies/were larger than our mortalities
And stories written in our stars change with every civilization that came
and left on stone a name,remained only while witnessed once
Forgotten like the flame of birth,and dying of ,and change
Night Sky Remains.

On My Way To The Winery

I met a man of dust-whose name was Shams
He was invisible to most
but his student Rumi saw him clearly
He was not of this world
but our world of wine ,laughter and dance
belonged to his expository generosities
Storyteller he,from West Texas
He would improvise jocular fictions
about men of sour grapes
angry men of Grapes of Wrath
Sufi Dancers whose steps
invoked the Divine in every smile
The journey was a long epic
Chapters of Longing for Refreshments
Flash fictions of Epiphanies
Mini-operas of Amazements
We were thoroughly engaged in the relationships between
longing and the Beloved.Vision and the Dream.
So we sat by Eternal Roadsides,sharing what we had both seen
If i could unfold his Map of Laughter/those ribald tales of drunken nights
How he started Green and ended up as Fine Wine
All is process,towards Perfection
All is taste and touch and bite
Never made it to that winery
But i keep feeling-
EVERY THING IS GOING TO BE ALL RIGHT!

SPIRIT THOM is an improvising bard who works best with improvising musicians.One of the founders of AUSTIN INTERNATIONAL POETRY FESTIVAL,and now available on ZOOM(Poetry Aloud!/SOAPBOX POETRY),SKYPE (Spoken n heard @Kick Butt) and CISCO WEBEX(Nomads Choir).Many clips on YOUTUBE.enjoy LIVE!Has performed with GONG,MOTHER GONG,KANGAROO MOON,FUTURE NOW,INVISIBLE OPERA COMPANY OF TIBET ,GLOSSO BABEL,TERATOMA,BLISSNINNIES etc etc etc

Katherine E. Young

Arlington, Virginia, Poet Laureate 2016-2018

hush: unbutton sunset

hush: unbutton sunset
let soft breeze skim your skin
on sidewalks people sigh
shake loose the day's last stone
from shoes that rub heels fine
buses abandon asphalt
to doze in antipodean lots
amid nimbi of razor wire

hush: unbutton sunset
unloose the coils of day
appointments at a quick-step
headlines deadlines red lights
hand-lettered signs
aligned in highway islands
amid the sea of vehicles
veteran—homeless—hungry

hush: unbutton sunset
fold back the flaps of evening
examine your ineffectual hands
scrolling through the pages
of mute anonymous faces
a man on hunger strike

a child warehoused in a cage
in a repurposed Walmart
adrift in the digital night

hush: unbutton sunset
dismiss your fear of the dark
in all the centuries
of our unlearning
we've saved only ourselves
and that only by the grace
of the god of small favors
and as twilight falls on the terrace
and ice melts in your glass
and your son comes for a kiss
to be wrapped in your arms and
carried to his air-conditioned room
you who believe in so little
must still believe in evening
enough to carry on

"hush: unbutton sunset" was written for the Columbia Pike Blues Festival by the Arlington (VA) Poet Laureate, a program of Arlington Cultural Affairs and Arlington Public Library.

Bar at the Folies-Bergère

It starts with the scent of lavender as she
buttons clean pantaloons, laces up stays,
smooths her bodice and shakes out the frills,
ties the black ribbon about her neck.
Her costume smells, as they all do: mingled
sweat and makeup, the fabric itself,
splashed, perhaps, with the licorice twist of absinthe.
Then come powder and rouge, the small earrings,
a pink and white corsage already starting
to droop. Her props are placed on view: beer bottles,
champagne, a vase containing two pale roses,
cut glass bowl of oranges that may
or may not indicate a certain kind
of availability. Leaning against
the marble bar, she doesn't look at you
(Why should she look at you? Can you give her
what she needs, or even cab fare home?):
posing, perhaps, or perhaps beyond posing,
her face bleak, artificially rosy amid
the moon-pale globes and crystals shimmering
in the ersatz heaven of the cabaret.
Perhaps a man inspects her in the glass,
perhaps he's looking past; neither of them
seems to see the woman on the trapeze,
feet squeezed into ankle boots of lizard green.
Later, she observes his red-gold lashes,
watches his still-young face slacken in sleep,
breathes in his scent of cigars, cheap brandy,
scent that clings to her fingers like orange oil

as she works her nails beneath the skin,
methodically stripping the pith to find
whatever's left of the fruit's sweet flesh.

"Bar at the Folies-Bergère" was commissioned by the Washington Shake-speare Theatre as part of its Poets are Present residency and appears in the Poets Are Present Anthology.

Katherine E. Young is the author of *Woman Drinking Absinthe*, *Day of the Border Guards* (2014 Miller Williams Arkansas Poetry Prize finalist) and two chapbooks. She is the editor of *Written in Arlington* and curator of *Spoken in Arlington*. Her poems have appeared in *Prairie Schooner*, *The Iowa Review*, *Subtropics*, and many others. She is the translator of *Look at Him* by Anna Starobinets, *Farewell, Aylis* by Azerbaijani political prisoner Akram Aylisli, and two poetry collections by Inna Kabysh. Young's translations of contemporary Russian-language poetry and prose have won international awards; several translations have been made into short films. Young was named a 2020 Arlington County (Virginia) Individual Artist Grant recipient, a 2017 National Endowment for the Arts translation fellow, and a 2015 Haw-thornden Fellow (Scotland). From 2016-2018, she served as the inaugural poet laureate for Arlington, Virginia. https://katherine-young-poet.com/

Aprilia Zank

Beat Poet Laureate, Germany

the digging of diamonds

in the nearly empty cinema
watching this film
again
with greasy tickets
torn at the corners
following
the digging of diamonds
from volcanic pipes
the vulture diving
peak stained with blood
the cry of torn silk
the bacchantes pour liquors
in goat shaped goblets
and the children perform
their tiny gig
their masks on
well after
the curtains were drawn
the dogs scratch at the door
and the diamonds burst
emerge in razor sharp
deep cutting sparks

Dr. Aprilia Zank is a lecturer for Creative Writing and Translation Theory from Germany. She is also a poet, a translator and the editor of several anthologies. She writes verse in English and German, and has been awarded several prizes. In 2018, she received the title "Dr. Aprilia Zank – Germany Beat Poet Laureate" from the National Beat Poetry Foundation.

Aprilia is also a passionate photographer.

About the Editor

James P. Wagner (Ishwa) is an editor, publisher, award-winning fiction writer, essayist, historian, actor, comedian, performance poet, and alum twice over (BA & MALS) of Dowling College. He is the publisher for Local Gems Poetry Press and the Senior Founder and President of the Bards Initiative. He is also the founder and Grand Laureate of Bards Against Hunger, a series of poetry readings and anthologies dedicated to gathering food for local pantries that operates in over a dozen states. His most recent individual collection of poetry is *Everyday Alchemy*. He was the Long Island, NY National Beat Poet Laureate from 2017-2019. He was the Walt Whitman Bicentennial Convention Chairman and has taught poetry workshops at the Walt Whitman Birthplace State Historic Site. James has edited over 100 poetry anthologies and hosted book launch events up and down the East Coast. He was named the National Beat Poet Laureate of the United States from 2020-2021. He is the owner/operator of The Dog-Eared Bard's Book Shop in East Northport, New York.

Made in the USA
Middletown, DE
06 June 2023

32156624R00199